Kerry Wood near his present home, with the Red Deer River in the background.

A LEGACY of LAUGHTER

Kerry Wood

Acknowledgements

The publisher wishes to acknowledge the continuing assistance of Alberta Culture, the Canada Council and the Alberta Foundation for the Literary Arts in the production of this book.

Special thanks are extended in the particular case of *A Legacy of Laughter* to the Alberta Recreation Parks and Wildlife Foundation.

The Foundation believes that the subject and quality of the book will contribute to a better understanding of the fragile beauty of all wildlife. The Foundation, in its support of this book is recognizing the life-long contribution of Kerry Wood, an eloquent and devoted Alberta conservationist.

A LEGACY of LAUGHTER

Kerry Wood

Illustrations by Jaime Romero

LONE
PINE

Kerry Wood
A Legacy of Laughter
Copyright © 1986 Kerry Wood and Lone Pine Publishing

First Printed 1986 5 4 3 2 1

Printed in Canada

The Publishers:
Lone Pine Publishing
414, 10357 109 Street
Edmonton, Alberta
T5J 1N3

Typesetting by Pièce de Résistance Typographers, Edmonton

Printed and Bound in Canada by Kromar Printing Ltd., Winnipeg, Manitoba

Canadian Cataloguing in Publication Data

Wood, Kerry, 1907-
A Legacy of Laughter

Autobiography

1. Wood, Kerry, 1907-   -childhood and youth. 2. Naturalists-Canada-biography. 3. Authors, Canadian (English)-20th century-Biography.
I. Title.

PS8545.047L43 1986   C813'.54   C86090136-X
PR9199.3.W66L43 1986

ISBN 0-919433-11-1

Dedicated to the
three Wood Chips
and the five Splinters

autographed by

Marjorie M. Wood

Kerry Wood.

Table Of Contents

Cover Design, Illustrations: Jaime Romero

Eggs and Charlie

Among the many useless skills learned while young was how to predict the sex of unborn creatures. It started when I read a news item about Japanese experts deciding the gender potential of eggs. At that time there were no members of the Rising Sun nation in our area, but Mr. Sammy Wong the Laundry man was my friend. We understood each other perfectly, though he spoke English with a Chinese accent and I spoke 'boy' at the time. He listened with solemn attention to my question, paused for reflection, then said:

"Use a piece of silk this long," he spread his hands. "You must tie something on the end, swing it sideways, then hold it over the egg. If the thing spins like this, it means male. This way, it's female."

"Mr. Wong, what's the something at the cord end?"

"Ahhh, that I do not know," he smiled at me. "You must discover the mystery for yourself."

His smooth ochre face crinkled in amusement when I pondered aloud that I did not know where to find a length of silk string, then inspiration came.

"Would a piece of green fishing line work?"

Mr. Wong looked doubtful, then phrased the question he had politely avoided from the first.

"Nobby, why do you wish to know?"

At the time I was a pre-teen, the youngest member of our family. Perhaps he also knew that none of us were in what was then referred to as a delicate condition. So I explained.

"I found a mallard's nest with eleven eggs in it just after reading of the Japanese knowing how to tell the sex of chicken eggs, and I've wondered how many nest eggs would turn into ducks and drakes."

An extra sparkle came into Mr. Wong's eyes, because he kept a pen of poultry behind his one-man laundry to supply himself with eggs and meat.

"If you learn, come back and tell me." Then his gleam of hope subsided as he added: "Nobby, I do not see how you can find out by examining wild duck eggs. When such eggs hatch, the little ones swim away with the mother. From then on she guards them in reed beds and I do not think you will be able to know them apart."

"I'm not interested in that part, Mr. Wong. All I want to know is how many different kinds of eggs there are, then I'll hunt for another mallard nest and test more eggs. By working around the shores of Gaetz Lakes, I might find four or five nests and learn what's the average difference. After that, I'll make notes in the scribbler where I keep track of nature things."

He nodded pleasantly and turned back to his steaming wash tubs, pausing long enough to say that he had enjoyed our talk.

• • •

If fishing string was a suitable alternative to a length of silk cord, and if a small pebble with a hole in it could be substituted for the secret device of the distant Japanese, the first mallard's nest contained eight duck eggs and three drakes. The proportion in the second was five ducks and four drakes. As I was approaching the third nest our town's senior naturalist, watching me through binoculars across the end of the lake, suddenly gave an enraged shout.

"Nobby! Come away from that nest at once! Come here!"

This was the voice of authority and I obeyed. Mr. Snell brushed aside my explanation and laced into me with a real tongue lashing.

"Don't you realize mallards might forsake their clutches because you handled their eggs?"

"I waited until the ducks had gone to feed before I went near."

"I heard one quacking an alarm. If you want to be a naturalist, you've got to shoulder responsibilities. Human scent scares wild things. Trappers even smoke their traps to destroy their hand smell. Haven't you read of that?"

"Yes, about animals—but do birds have a sense of smell?"

Charles H. Snell calmed down when he realized I was only trying to learn.

"Well—Yes, I think some birds do. Magpies, for example. Put out a piece of smelly meat and notice how quickly magpies and crows come to investigate. But scent or no scent, you've got to respect the privacy of duck nests. This Gaetz Lakes region is a bird sanctuary and you mustn't violate the rules."

"No, sir," I said meekly. "Yet I like knowing where ducks build. From now on, I'll try to learn by watching. Will that be all right?"

"I suppose so, though I'd not like you to tell any of your young friends about nest locations."

"I won't. I once told a boy about a yellow warbler's nest and he nearly spilled out the eggs trying to look. Since then I haven't told anyone where nests are, except Sid."

Mr. Snell smiled, knowing that his son Sid and I were chums. Our friendship was cemented more firmly when he let me look through his binoculars to admire the spectacular spring plumage of a shoveller drake. He identified a number of wildflowers and a soapalallie shrub, nodded approval when I drew his attention to heron tracks on a mud flat, and actually beamed when I located a blue jay's twig nest on a low spruce. When we emerged from the woodlands to the proper road, he generously offered to help me solve any of my nature problems in the future.

Reaching home, I remembered a robin's nest built on a board

shelf. This particular Ma Robin had an extra white mark on a wing feather which made her easy to identify. If she raised the brood in our back yard where worm gathering was a snap, perhaps her fledglings would hang around long enough for me to tell how they turned out. After she had gone to feed, I climbed a step ladder to swing my fishing line and pebble over each egg in turn. If my apparatus worked, there was an equal balance of two eggs of each sex.

Another notion popped into mind. We did not keep any cats, partly because my mother could not tolerate their odour, mostly because our family enjoyed having wild birds nearby and cats and birds don't mix. However, there was a friend whose home was down in the town valley who had mentioned that their mother cat was due.

"Has she kittened yet?" I asked him that evening.

"Naw, not yet. D'you want one when they come?"

"Nope. But if you'll bring her outside, I'll tell you how many kinds she's going to have."

He looked at me in that peculiar way my associates among the boy population regarded me when they heard about my new notions. Yet without further argument he got the mother-to-be and held her still while I brought out my fragment of fishline and pebble. I twirled it and held the swinging stone over the charmed cat who tried her best to bat down the tantalizing object. The pebble spun wildly and gave my wrist a painful jolt.

"Well, whaddayuh say?"

"It didn't turn out like I expected. All I know for sure is, she'll have a mixture."

"I knew that already," he scoffed, releasing the cat. Since I was down in the valley already and Mr. Wong's place of business was only two blocks farther on, I called to report on the day's experiments. He commented favourably on the imbalance in the two mallard nests, and nodded gravely when I recounted my scolding from Mr. Snell. Mr. Wong laughed when told about my wrist getting jerked by the spin over my friend's cat.

"Oh, and there's a robin nesting on our house shelf. If my pebble works, she's going to hatch two of each."

He had me describe how I had accomplished the test by holding out one egg at a time and twirling the string and rock with the other hand. My oriental mentor studied me thoughtfully, stopped his work, and said:

"Come."

Mr. Wong led me through his neat living quarters out to the chicken run and coop. Speaking softly in his musical language, he coaxed a broody hen off a dozen brown eggs and held them out, one at a time, for me to perform my ritual. He seemed pleased when I predicted five roosters and seven hens.

"They will make good meals," he murmured, carefully replacing the willing hen on the setting before we returned to the front of his shop where he was ironing men's shirts. "I will keep track of her young and let you know how they turn out. Nobby, come again soon."

It became a habit to drop in on Mr. Wong. I took him Scottish oat cakes from our home, receiving in return sweet oblongs of white-powdered ginger. Once I spoke of the fishing fun I enjoyed so much along the Red Deer River; after much hesitation, he asked if I ever caught more fish than our family needed. Of course! We had been friendly enough before, but after my first gift of fish, I was certain to see a welcoming smile on Mr. Wong's handsome round face every time we met.

The special pebble was lost and for years I forgot my curiosity about mallard eggs. That useless bit of knowledge was stored in the back part of whatever brain I possessed until—Lo! I became a married man and three years later, my lovely wife informed me of the gladsome tidings of our parental prospects.

"I wonder what it'll be?" Marjorie mused.

A snippet of fishline was easily found, though not a pebble with a convenient hole in it. However, there happened to be unshelled peanuts in a bowl on our table. A reef was knotted around the waist of one and I swung it sideways before holding it over Marjorie's middle.

"A girl!" I announced.

"That'll be just fine," Marjorie smiled.

On the three occasions when there were reasons to twirl the fishline, the method proved infallible. We joked about this to an older married pair who already had their family quota. The man was intrigued by my streak of lucky intuition.

"Come outside," he invited. "I've had a dowser walk over my farm yard and he told me where to dig for a new well. There are four water seams around here. I'll cut you a forked branch and let you have a go at finding them."

"What's a dowser?"

"A well-witcher. You've heard of witching a well?"

"Yes, but I didn't know they had a special name."

"Yup. Dowsers use willow." He rummaged in a nearby clump and returned with a smooth-barked piece of osier in a Y shape. "Hold it like this, then walk with the point out in front. Grip the ends tightly and go strolling around in any direction. We'll see what happens."

It was uncanny to feel the bark twist away from the green-cut willow stick, wrenching in spite of my firm and resisting grip. The point of the Y turned down at three of the four locations which the experienced dowser had previously located.

I do not challenge the preternatural ability some people have in selecting well sites, a few even able to give actual depths where water may be found, but never again will I try the stunt. The forceful movements of that willow wand were completely beyond my control. My inward feelings of helplessness during those scary moments on that evening long ago convinced me to avoid such mysterious rites forever.

Yet it was good fun to know in advance the outcome of our own family hatchings, and also to remember that Mr. Sammy Wong told me I had been accurate in predicting the sex of the poultry eggs.

• • •

I tried to learn useful things too. My brother Charlie always put a padlock on his tool chest which contained the family hammer, saw, and chisels, therefore most of my early 'makings' were knife-manufactured and crude. When Charlie got out his tools to make something, I hovered nearby and envied his expertise. He has always been one of those geniuses who can mend an egg-beater, fix a leaking tap, or take apart three abandoned bicycles and produce a shiny like-new model from the spare pieces. When rumour reached Red Deer, in those dinosaur days of our youth, that a miraculous thing called radio had been invented, my brother sent off for tubes and wires, put them inside a small box, attached an assortment of knobs and told us that the thingamajig worked. The family assembled around a single set of earphones and listened to squeals, stutterings, faint nasal voices and tinny music originating from an American station over a thousand miles away from our location in Central Alberta. All of us were impressed but Charlie, who sold the set to a lucky member of eager prospects, sent away for better tubes and constructed a larger set that brought in programs much more clearly.

As a young man, Charlie became the engineer in charge of the first radio broadcasting station in our district during the booming late Twenties. He fiddled smoothly with an impressive array of dials and activated a microphone to speak the call letters, CKLC, and was quite sorry when the company folded in 1933 as the depression grew worse. He and his wife Geneva and daughter Doris moved to Lethbridge where Charlie became the engineer of another station that did not collapse. Eventually he became the fix-it man for a Calgary company dealing in high quality electric organs. Salesmen travelled all over the province and coaxed church people to give up pipe and foot-pumped organs in favour of these more versatile and compact instruments. They were financed easily—Oh, how easily!—on the time payment plan. Sometimes when a new organ was trucked in, carried carefully into the revered space allotted, connected to power and the keyboard rippled in anticipation, something would go wrong and it would refuse to respond.

"Send Charlie," the harassed salesman would urge the Calgary office.

There were many hundreds of parts in the new organ, most

of which my brother got to know on an I-see-you-at-last basis. He would spread them out along the seats of adjacent pews and carpeted church aisles, then go back inside to search for more. The hand-wringing minister and a few of the more solvent members of his flock would be poised on the outskirts of the multifarious parts, inwardly questioning their own wisdom in parting with the old reliable pumper to take on this beautiful but temperamental new gadget for which they had collectively signed on the dotted line.

"It'll work fine in a few minutes," the worried salesman would volunteer. "Trust Charlie. He knows."

Meanwhile, Charlie would not have the foggiest notion of what was wrong at that particular moment, but he kept removing items until he located something that was either loose or not attached properly. Once it was a strand of wire no thicker than a hair from a bald man's pate, but it crossed another in some manner that made the organ squeal like a tormented banshee. At last satisfied he had found and fixed the offending part, Charlie would reassemble the organ bit by bit, replace the handsome woodwork that hid all practical workings, and finally step around to the keyboard. Once he was seated in front it was no grandly sounding chord that came soulfully out, but a brisk rendition of a sacreligious tune—the only piece of music he had learned to finger.

He tried to tell me how those organs worked when I went to watch him mend a locally installed instrument. Charlie pressed in one peg and out came flute-like sounds that got a couple of robins excited out on the churchyard trees. In my pleasure over this distraction, I failed to understand how the electric current vibrated through something and all the exquisite sound came from over yonder.

"Two speakers for a completely balanced sound," Charlie explained. "It's quite simple."

When he played his naughty tune on the guitar version of the organ instead of the flute, the robins outside lost interest and went back to hunting worms. I turned again to my brother and expressed some enthusiasm for the organ. Yes, I was much impressed by the variety of instruments at the beck and call of any keyboard master;

indeed, the organ could be turned into something resembling a muted piano if it was required for a vocal accompaniment. Truly I did try to comprehend what Charlie was telling me, because among other writing commitments at the time, I was submitting a weekly newspaper column of 'general interest' and at the moment I urgently needed a new idea. With only a faint savvy of the organ's workings but most awed by its musical abilities, we drove to my home where Charlie supped tea and cakes with Marjorie and the children as I pounded the typewriter and blithely wrote of him and the electric organ.

Not too much about organs, true enough, but a lot about my brother. He had received telephone calls in Calgary in the midst of the slumbering hours and he had to drive miles to where a shattered salesman had installed one of their splendid new marvels. These emergencies usually happened late on Saturday nights, just before a magnificent program was due to be featured at the Sunday morning worship hour. Once it was a loose shingle on the church roof that had allowed a drip during a thunder storm. The water penetrated a crack at the back of the organ, diverted along a rod and short-circuited something which turned the scheduled hymns into bellowing gasps resembling a circus calliope with a hacking cough. Charlie used sandpaper on the rusted parts after tracing the leak with the aid of a hastily summoned roofer, then put everything back together again. Out rang his raucous test piece at midnight until the insulted organist insisted on taking over and made George Frederick Handel's music sweeten the soured atmosphere.

Another time it was a hungry church mouse that gnawed through the coverings of a wire and made one of J.S. Bach's fugues sound like the loneliest rose of summer sans foliage as well as bloom. At still another town a janitor got interested in viewing the inner arrangements and took off the easily removed back, then left a quarter of a ham sandwich inside when his curiosity had been satisfied. Charlie said that organ sounded worse than a coyote with yodelling problems. The minister and elders were abashed to be shown the mouldering remains of the sandwich reposing on some important feature, even more taken aback when Charlie, forgetful of their august presences, fingered his fast way through his impertinent tune. "The main thing is, it worked again." One of his most rewarding repair jobs happened on a Sunday morning in a church about forty miles from home. The congregation was present in all their finery, the choir girls looked lovely; Charlie thought one blonde in particular appeared to be positively angelic. The local clergyman and a visiting minister were pompously decorous in their black robes, though both looked vulnerable and disadvantaged as they stood on floor level down from the elevated pulpit. Only Charlie, hatless out of respect, breathless because of haste, seemed quite sure of himself as he experimentally pressed the dead keys and hustled around to the rear of the instrument. In a surprisingly brief time he returned to the keyboard, poised his fingers above it to play his infamous test tune—then realized all the people had on their reverently composed faces, the choir girls were beatific in their uniformed piety, the two clerics now trying to wear high-sky countenances. All might be terribly upset if he played his usual number. Instead, Charlie allowed his fingers to stray slowly over the now operational keys and foot-touched some of the harmonizing pedals.

"If I do say so myself, what came out sounded like a decently churchified refrain. I was doing just fine until the gray-haired organist lady asked me to name the composer."

Charlie quickly got off the bench and ushered her onto it.

"I said it was 'the fourteenth bar of Mood-ah-lallie-off-skewer's Twenty-eighth Recessional'. She smiled at me and said she had just recalled the rest of that beautiful phrase and was tempted to change her morning's program and put it in."

The much-relieved reverend in charge put a compelling hand on Charlie's arm and led him out a side door, smack into the middle of a cemetery. He shook hands with my brother and told him he had saved their day, thanking him profusely for being such an efficient technician.

"I didn't think it would help any to explain that their cleaning lady must have mopped the floor too vigorously back of the organ, because all that was wrong was that the electrical connection had been yanked out. I don't know what the company charged the church for that emergency service call, but I do remember getting a bonus in my pay cheque for working overtime.''

All this went into my column, which was published in due course. Charlie telephoned to say he had laughed loud and long when he read my attempts to explain the capabilities of the wondrous instrument, yet the next time I was in Calgary my brother thought the column put him under an obligation to treat me to a luncheon at a café. Purée Mongol was the featured soup of the day and I asked him what it was.

''Oh, that! The cooks just hunt around for a man from high Asia, scrub him clean, and make soup out of him. I suggest we order the lamb chops.''

The Tumbles

One of the many mistakes of boyhood happened in the bullrush muck of Second Lake at the Sanctuary. My curiosity had been aroused by the large number of red-winged blackbird nests suspended among the green rushes near the southern shore.

"I'll wade in and count them," and forthwith stripped off shoes, stockings, and clumsy knee britches of the period. Clad only in cap, shirt, and underwear shorts, I ventured out to explore. There were chirping alarms of red-wings, while coots, grebes and ducks contributed dismayed comments about the invasion. A number of warblers, thrushes, a catbird and a passing marsh hawk joined in with an assortment of protests. All of which should have warned me off, but my initial count had already revealed nine nests. Eagerly I extended the search farther, my legs sinking to the thighs in slimy ooze. Just as I reached over to look into another red-wing cradle, a bittern cackled and exploded suddenly from nearby rushes.

In whirling to see the magnificent bird, I lost my balance and plunged headlong into sticky water. As I gasped to the surface and struggled to regain footing, lake floor vegetation yielded under my thrashing and I sank waist deep. Floundering in panic, I lost all interest in blackbird nests as I ploughed mud-heavy step after step toward land. Before reaching the boggy security of shore, a buried

root tripped me and there was another dismal immersion into the stinking weeds.

"My clothes!"

Everything on me was filthy and from the waist down I was coated in chocolate-coloured slime. There was even a streamer of clammy weeds draped over one shoulder. After wiping my hands clean on dry grass, I gathered up pants, stockings and shoes and sought higher ground and more seclusion than the beach afforded. So far as I knew no one else was in the Sanctuary at the moment, but with a boy's modesty I sought privacy before stripping.

"My mother'll scalp me," I thought, remembering her oft-repeated admonition that clothes did not grow on trees. To make matters worse, this was my town outfit. There had been an errand of delivering potato scones to our friend Mrs. Christy McKenzie before I had diverted over to the Gaetz Lakes that day. Now my destination was a hillside spring, a basin-sized pool fringed with pink wintergreen, Calypso and fly-specked orchids. Gingerly I picked a bare-footed path upward on scratchy spruce needles, soon reaching the twin-flowered place where the clear water had formed a small pool. Using handfuls of moss as wash-cloths, I was able to scrub my body partially clean. But cap, shirt, and underpants were another matter. Rinse after rinse did nothing to rid them of slough smell and yellow stains. Finally it seemed best to admit defeat. They were spread on sunny bushes to half-dry before I donned the limp things and went ruefully home. Not only my soiled appearance, but my guilty expression caught my mother's immediate attention.

"Whit's a-miss?" she demanded. When details of the accident had been related, she clucked her anger. "Ye daft laddie, ye might ha'e been droon't all by yerself doon there. Last night ye telt me wild birrrds need tae be left alone tae thrive, mind? Weel, why d'ye no' heed yer ain advice?" She dropped her scolding tone. "Noo tak' towel, soap, and hot watter frae the stove reservoir into yer room and strip, get clean, and come back wi' all the dirrrty things when ye've put on chore clothes. It'll be scrub boarrd wurrrk fer you, laddie, and ye'll never learrrn aboot washin' clothes ony younger."

Not even a cuff on the ear, which had been the least of my expectations. She took over the washing after the rough cleansing, talking about her own aversion to 'dookin' as she called swimming. My father had enjoyed long swims in Scottish seas and lochs and now in our Red Deer River whenever he got the chance, but she had never shared his enthusiasm for it. I had already learned that swimming was difficult for me, except for enough dog-paddle strokes for safety's sake to retrieve fishing lures when they got hung up. Many of my school chums were experts at the Big Tree hole or out on river backwaters, but I shared in every boy's delight in the wild exuberance of splashing through the deep Cronquist Rapids. After a few trips through those benign rollers, a driftwood fire on shore warmed our chilled bodies. Yet we had to be wary around those fires, because close at hand were layers of limestone. If some joker tossed a fragment of that gray rock into a fire, next moment there would be an explosion and pieces of flying rock and hot ashes stung our naked bodies.

• • •

Much later, my friend Sid Snell had an idea concerning watersports.

"I found a plan for making what's called a 'quick' canoe."

This was after adulthood and I had started courting the delightful Marjorie. Paddling a graceful canoe downriver to her family's streamside farm conjured up a romantic picture, so I was eagerly receptive to Sid's suggestion.

"We can build it in Dad's garage," he added.

We bought the materials and got to work in our spare time. Instead of having closely spaced ribs across the body, five forms were placed in that position. A series of full length slats of cedar formed the overall shape of the craft. The artist's conception of the finished article was attractively beguiling in the magazine spread, but our skeleton frame looked alarmingly flimsy until canvas was snugged overtop. We asked a local painter about a finish coat. His advice might have been excellent for house walls, but it proved disastrous for sealing canvas. We lugged our quickie along short-cut paths to the Sanctuary and launched on First Lake. Everything was fun until the water began seeping in, then we went ashore and hoisted the now heavily soaked craft onto our shoulders and staggered the long portage back to the Snell garage.

"I'll skip going down the winding river miles to Marjorie's place, because we'd need a four-horse team to haul our quickie home!"

• • •

Mr. J.J. Gaetz's 230 acres of wild woodland had been one of my favourite haunts since our family's arrival in town. It was under a mile from our hilltop home, slightly farther than the convenient haven of the Bower Woods where beavers had many dams across Waskasoo creek. I spent many spare hours in both locations, often seeking new vistas or different trails in each, sometimes squatting in a natural blind to wait for the wild things to resume their activities around me. At Gaetz Lakes the wider expanse of water attracted a larger variety of species from loons down to staccato-voiced marsh wrens whose moated nests often eluded me. Assorted rails uttered their distinctive cries from the reed beds, birds seldom seen but often heard. Muskrats were plentiful in early years, and their feeding cruises etched waves that rippled in slow Vees across the water's surface. Near a log tangle on one shore I saw the furtive movements of swift little animals Mr. Gaetz called beaver mice; later on these were found to be water shrews.

There was a radiance of wildflowers throughout the Sanctuary, always an abundance of summer butterflies—the elegant swallowtails of spring, brown fritillaries hovering on midsummer's brown-eyed susans, Camberwell Beauties liking the goldenrods of autumn, with blues, skippers, clear-wings, and ghost moths somewhere in between. Often after school I detoured over to Gaetz Lakes and loitered there in happy fascination of its many wonders, until the inner prod of duty sent me racing home to milk Bessie and feed our chickens.

"Whit did ye see this time?" my mother asked after I had panted in to change for choring.

"A yellow-bellied sapsucker, a snipe's nest on a grassy hummock, and different tracks on the shore mud. Maybe made by a mink."

"Aweel, that's fine." She handed me a scalded milk pail and became practical. "I've checked oor cream pans, an' there'll be enough to mak' a big churnin' fer Saturday morn."

Up and down I plied the smooth-handled tool with its crossed end, tediously thumping it in the earthenware crock until a change of feel announced that the thick cream had separated into butter and buttermilk. My reward was the first drink of the tart fluid, while my mother used a large wooden basin and curved wooden paddles to squeeze out all excess moisture. There were mold patterns to form the butter into shape for table and cooking use. Only on rare occasions could our family coax her to let us have fresh cream as a covering for a special dessert, such as a feed of wild strawberries.

During those lengthy, house-bound times of churning, I pondered the enchantments of Mr. Gaetz's sanctuary. He sometimes loosed a few head of cattle there and now and then he allowed an Indian family to camp on the gravelly hump between the two lakes. The wilderness acres had not been part of his original 1885 homestead, yet he so admired the beauties of the adjacent land that he eventually bought it from the Metis owner. From then on, the park-like gem was preserved almost undisturbed by man.

"The Indians didn't do any harm there," he once told me. "All they wanted was a quiet place to camp for a day or two between rounds of visiting town fairs. Most of them I knew personally, the older ones having helped me clear poplar and willow scrub from my farm fields."

Mrs. Gaetz added a gleeful memory of Jack Gaetz's kindness to Indian campers. Whenever a family of natives were tented on the gravelled land, he saw to it that they had vegetables from his garden and store-bought meat. It happened that Mr. Gaetz was also a staunch Liberal, and if any dignitaries of that party visited Red Deer they were hospitably entertained at the Gaetz home.

"One time Jack came back from town with half a dozen important party men for an afternoon's yarning and supper, and he brought two parcels from the meat market. He handed me one and had our hired man carry the other down to the Indian camp. As I prepared supper, I secretly censored his enthusiasm for politics because he had been remiss in his shopping duties. But when I served the big stew to his party friends, Jack looked across the table at me and said: 'The parcels got mixed. Well, the Indians have some mighty fine roasts for their meal tonight'."

While the churning plunger went up and down, the conception of preserving land for the purpose of protecting nature raised a copycat idea in my young head. Could it be done here at home? We were renters at the time, which did not prevent us from having lots of bird boxes around and offering food titbits to the tamer creatures both summer and winter.

Many years later Marjorie and I owned seven acres to share with our wild neighbours at our first homesite. We installed benches in sheltered nooks from where we could enjoy watching the purple martins, tree swallows and bluebirds in boxes, catch many glimpses of warblers and vireos above and behind our brush-screened locations, and marvel at hummingbirds probing nasturtium trumpets for nectar. In cold weather lumps of beef suet brought friendly chickadees, nuthatches, and salt-and-pepper woodpeckers to dine. Sometimes we despaired of saucy blue jays monopolizing our feeders, not only the fatty prizes but the window shelf itself where bread crumbs and boxes of canary seed were sprinkled. Dainty redpolls clustered on the seeds some winters, also noisy and showy-feathered evening grosbeaks. Their cousins, the shyer pine grosbeaks, often followed the gathering bird crowds to our place out of curiosity, then the rosy males provided us with musical serenades.

"Where did you lose your cap?" Marjorie asked one day early in our marriage as we started down the steep hill toward town. "Was it near here?"

My people had moved away from the family home, leaving

me to 'batch' alone in a cabin and learn my trade of writing for juvenile magazines. There came a minor scare in the winter. I had spent a week preparing a manuscript, plotted by pencil, proofed and scratched up three or four times for improvement before transferring the carefully typed words to bond paper. A stamped return envelope was enclosed, name of editor and magazine properly addressed on the outer kraft, and I had set off for town to mail it one evening. As I descended into the darker shadows of the tall spruces, my tweed cap whirled off my head in startling fashion and I spun around, half expecting this to be a hidden friend's prank. No one was there. Puzzled, I turned and saw my cap lying askew beside the path. There was no overhanging branch near enough to have touched me, no plausible explanation for the mishap. However, no harm had been done. I replaced the cap on my head and continued on towards the post office, still with a strong glow of hope about my story's eventual reception at a magazine office in far away New York City.

A week later when I walked the same trail at twilight, my cap was snatched from my head a second time. I caught a fleeting glimpse of a great horned owl. One of its talons had torn through the tweed and bright red blood spurted from my then thickly thatched skull.

"I'll give it a scare."

Next day a small rectangle of wood was wrapped with rabbit fur and a screw eye fastened on, to which I tied a generous length of fishing line. As evening approached the decoy was placed at the strategic spot on the path, the string paid out toward a screen of small spruces where I sat to wait. After dusk the owl swooped in noiselessly and settled itself on top of a high stump. There was a long interval of tense expectancy, but at last the four-note hoot boomed out and I tugged the string. When the furry stick rustled, the owl swooped. The second its claws closed on the lifeless wood, the bird released the bait and circled back up to the tower. There was a ruffling of plumage, a long time of peering around, followed by a period of quiet before its beak opened.

"Ka-hoo-hoo-hoo!"

I made the stick jump and at once the owl pounced. Again the bait was dropped. This time the bird doubled back over the spot, its large head turned as it glared down at the tantalizing object. Perhaps it had expected the sudden hooting to startle a rabbit from its form, cause a sleeping bird to stir on a branch, or at the very least disclose the rustle of a mouse. Back it went to the stump top. After many more ploys, the time came when the frustrated bird clutched the innocent stick tightly and started to carry it away. I gave the string a tremendous jerk which caused the owl to flip-flop in mid-air. It nearly somersaulted to earth before its pumping wings managed to right the body. I jumped from my hide-out and yelled. At that the bird sped away like a frightened gray ghost. Back through the darkness came a short hoot, almost a question. I shouted again. Mr. Owl did not forget my lesson; it kept away from that particular watchtower and there were no more cap snatchings until a much later time and a different owl.

"Yes, it happened near here," I answered Marjorie. "The cat-owl's stump fell years ago, perhaps I used it for firewood when batching. Yonder is the stand of spruce where I hid with the string— see, they're no longer small, but half-grown now."

"I wonder if the owl we heard hooting last night is a descendant of your head-scratcher?"

"Maybe, but as yet, no bad habits to annoy us."

Later that week when we were crossing a pasture field at dusk, against the sunset sky we saw the new owl swoop from a tree and sink its talons into the rump of a horse that had switched its tail. There was a squeal of pain, and a frantic galloping by the slightly punctured horse as the owl flapped off in the opposite direction.

"Perhaps it'll go back to its nest and brag about the big one that got away," laughed Marjorie. "Just like you do, when you go fishing."

We wondered if great horned owls hunt on the theory that if it moves, it must be edible.

• • •

This summer day of 1985 we used a broom to sweep out the birds' paddling pool, wiped it clean, then ran fresh water from the 310-foot well. Even through the rubber hose we could feel the chill of that water. When seven pails had been emptied into the large galvanized pan, we retreated houseward to watch from a window. A white-throated sparrow was the first bird back. It had been having baths at intervals all morning in the shallower, sun-warmed water before we had made the change. Now it landed at the rim of the deep end, plunged in confidently, uttered a shriek of alarm and fluttered the full length of the icy water to the shallow end. It flew with con-siderable wet-feather difficulty. But it persisted and went to the top of the birch tree where its shrill protests soon turned into the silver serenade so beloved by Canadians, who call it the Canada bird.

By mid afternoon the sun had heated the water and half a dozen juncoes, two goldfinches, and a yellow warbler had drinks and social baths together in the pan. One of the numerous Pa Robins of the region came to flounce in. He splashed about with so much vigor that the flying spray forced the smaller birds to yield up the whole paddling pool to his happy ablutions.

Later Marjorie and I went out to refill the sunflower seed tumbler, spread more handfuls of wild bird seeds on the shelf, and sprinkle another ration of bread crumbs. We listened to wheezy notes of cedar waxwings, the name call of a rufous-sided towhee, saw a Traill's flycatcher teeter on the far stretch of the clothesline, and heard a Swainson's hawk screech querulously from a distant sky. Back indoors again, we wondered if our thousands of trees and shrubs, two open fields, a sunny ravine slope, 40 acres of land and a half mile of river frontage partially copied John Jost Gaetz's marvelous idea of a wildlife sanctuary.

The Potato Year

My father wrote regularly, if briefly, to my mother during his travels west, north, and east of Edmonton in the early years.

> *Dear Liz:*
> *I will be in these towns*
> *on dates given.*
> *(List of towns and dates.)*
> *Hope all well,*
> *Willie.*

My mother told me I must write to him once a week at an appropriate address, advising him about my progress at school or lack of it, any nature happening I wished to share, then sign it and address the envelope.

"Do I have to sign my real name?"

My chums called me Nobby, because the family dog of the same name had bushy eyebrows similar to mine.

"Aye, ye're never tae sign 'Nobby' tae yer fayther. Oor dug doesna' write letters."

In due course there would come from some small town the following reply:

> *Dear Son:*
>
> *Yours noted. Be sure to take*
> *secateurs and cut all seed*
> *heads off our lilacs.*
> *Hope all well.*
> *Wm, C. Wood.*

I do not remember receiving any letter from him ending with a mention of the fact that he was my loving father, though in his quiet way it was obvious that Wm. C. Wood was very fond of his two remaining sons. My father was then working as a 'roadman' for the *Edmonton Bulletin* newspaper, which sent him travelling to small towns within the radius of the *Bulletin's* circulation. There he visited public schools during noon hours or after classes to appoint local carriers for the paper. He returned home from one of those larger rural towns in the Peace River block and told us of his satisfaction with one elderly 'boy,' a retarded man of 30 who had been a diligent *Bulletin* carrier for nine years and had banked every penny earned. The man proudly showed my father his bank book to prove that he had piled up over $2,000 during his tenure of service.

"Twa thoosand!" my mother marvelled at the fortune. "Just once, I'd like tae get my hands on money like that."

"Perhaps in time," my father placated her soothingly, although later, when helping me select an oat sheef for the cow he confessed with a wry smile that we were never likely to accumulate much money. "We Woods haven't got the Midas touch," and a chuckle came from behind his Van Dyke whiskers. "The only legacy you'll inherit from us is the ability to laugh."

Yet in all our long years of association, I never heard him laugh heartily. Smiles and chuckles often enough, while on many occasions his shoulders literally shook with mirth as he shared a joke with the family, frequently after he had found something amusing in books. There were moments when his absorption with books created awkward situations for me when he was at home on a school day.

I had rushed the one mile home to sup hot soup or perhaps a steaming bowl of tripe and onions, but just when I bundled up again to trot back to the House of Learning my father would halt me as I headed for the door.

"Listen to this," and he would read a passage from whatever volume had intrigued him. On one happy occasion it was an excerpt from Jerome K. Jerome's *Three Men in a Boat*. The following weekend I buried myself in the book and it became a favourite.

"Let the laddie run alang," my mother would intervene on my behalf whenever he read to me during school noontimes. She protested too on Saturday mornings when I had been given a specific amount of money and the family grocery list to do the shopping downtown. This was to save her from venturing out into the bitter weather when frosty air bothered her breathing. "He's tae get oor week's supplies, and if ye keep bletherin' awa' at him, dinner'll be late-cooked this day."

Still, if he was much impressed by whatever volume held his enthusiasm at the moment, my father might reach for his coat, hat, and gloves and accompany me. He often crowded me off the narrow path through the deep snow in his single-minded eagnerness to push at me some highlight of prose or poetry. Once we reached the business section he let me attend to mundane shopping while he waited at one side. Before we headed for home sharing the parcel load, he coaxed me to get him another book from the public library. I thought it odd that he never personally patronized the library, though he gave me detailed instructions as to what kinds I should borrow on his account. From his travels he brought home books picked up in second-hand stores. The wide variety of his reading, mostly in the classic vein, had influenced his mode of speech. Though there was a definite burring sound to his speaking voice inherited from Scotland, he never lapsed into the colorful dialect which so endeared my mother's broad tongue to all.

"Fillin' his head wi' all they fancy quotes," she once scolded, yet with a hint of pride in her tone. "Ye'll not gi'e him time fer lookin' at his birds!"

He approved of illustrations in P.E. Taverner's *Birds of Eastern Canada*, which was then the only available reference dealing with my hobby. On occasion he listened amiably enough whenever I became ecstatic over some new discovery among the species thriving near home. If at the moment he chanced to be on his outside bench having a smoke, he sat with one leg crossed over a knee and swaying to an inward rhythm. Perhaps he would apply another match to the cold pipe, then puff contentedly while he listened to my rhapsodies about finding a brown thrasher's nest. As he heard my description of the cinnamon-coloured bird's songs and imitations, he might allow his briar to go out. Before we returned indoors, he flapped his jacket so the smoke smell would not linger on his clothing to upset my mother's sensitive bronchial tubes. Once reaching his special chair, invariably he buried himself in reading material.

Once for a few months he followed the richly embroidered literature of India in translation, another time he sampled the philosophies of John Stuart Mill. When he was deep in the Mill treatise he would read a chapter at a time, put a hand to his brow in thoughtful meditation while he stared into space, then set the volume aside momentarily to reach for some well-thumbed book of poetry.

"All they lang verses," my mother lamented one day during a pause when he looked up to see what was going on. "All they small printed lang verses, and ye dinna tak' time tae learrrrn the wurrrds o' Loch Lomond."

"Why should I be worried about the high road or the low road when the middle one's much the smoothest?"

"Noo, dinna go twistin' meanin's away frae me, Willie. Tell me plain, d'ye ken the wurrrds?"

"I should. I've heard you singing them often enough."

"Say them oot, line after line."

He would hide a smile behind a hand, clear his throat, seem about to recite the old song, then look at her quizzically and utter his one exclamation.

"Pshaw!"

"Dinna 'Shaw' me, Willie Wood. I can tell ye've clean forgot the wurrrrds tae Loch Lomond.''

These verbal sparring matches were their way of showing affection for one another. Throughout my boyhood years I never heard them exchange words of endearment, but their devotion to each other was there all the time. Charlie and I felt secure in its stability, for them and for us. Long ago we had accepted the fact that ours was not a demonstrative family. Indeed, the first time I remember my mother giving me a hasty kiss on the cheek was as she was boarding a train, Vancouver bound, at the breakup of our family home into different locations. Nor was the gesture important to her at that moment, because her chief concern was to give me final instructions about living alone, or 'batching'.

''Cook yer food proper, keep yersel' clean always, gang early tae bed an' rise wi' the dawn—Oh, and keep yer mind busy.''

• • •

Of course, that was off in what appeared to be a distant future. What excited me during the winter of my eleventh year was the near approach of Christmas. Boys at school were talking tall nonsense about lavish presents they expected to get from their parents. That aspect of the approaching holiday never bothered me, as our gifts were on a definite schedule and known in advance. An orange each and a pair of woollen mittens knitted by my mother, a book from my father, a craft article from Charlie, while they got whittled tokens from me made of diamond willow. The truly fascinating puzzle of the season was which of our flock of two dozen poultry would be sacrificed to provide the feast? I liked our rooster, a pompous bird all buff-orange ruffled feathers with fringes of black on wing tips and tail. He was a chanticleer jaundiced of eye, also cruel of beak if my hand strayed near while filling the flock's water pan or distributing feed for his clucking harem. Many a peck that yellow curved bill dealt out, yet I still liked the vain strutter and admired his lusty crowing inside the winter coop or out in the limitations of the screened run whenever a thaw moderated the hard weather. More especially I enjoyed him when his robust roof-top bragging took place in open range times of spring, summer, and autumn when he arrogantly challenged all of poultry-dom to exceed his loudest boast of superiority.

"Na, it'll no' be oor rooster," my mother reassured me about the forthcoming Christmas meal. "D'ye ken which hen has stoppit layin'?"

I was reluctant to point a fatal finger at any. Looking after the chickens was my responsibility, mostly because my father broke out in sores if his hands came in contact with feathers. This excused him from the duty of setting the broody hens in spring and from bothersome decisions about choosing victims for our rare feeds of chicken. While it was up to me to select pot birds, Charlie had the dastardly task of decapitating the unfortunate hens, plucking them bald and the messy chore of extracting the entrails.

"It's his way of getting out of it," Charlie confided to me one time when he was in the midst of the smelly cleaning job.

"No, it isn't. I saw blisters all over his hands, last time he tried to pluck."

"He claims to be too tender-hearted to stand the blood," Charlie went on. "Our Pa's smart, the way he gets out of all the nasty stuff. Maybe he's just plain lazy."

We both fell silent, abashed as we recalled our first three seasons on that hilltop acreage. My parents had rented four parcels of pasture land, each about an acre in size, had them ploughed and harrowed, then planted the whole area in potatoes. Charlie helped after his electrical work down in the town, and I joined in after school and every weekend. My father had always been a lean person in physical stature, but during those rushed days of hoeing the holes, carrying out pailfuls of seed potatoes, dropping them into the ready spaces, then going back row after row to cover and rake the soil smooth, he became positively gaunt with fatigue.

"Och, Willie," my mother scolded softly as he dozed over the meal in the kitchen. "Ye'll need tae keep up yer strength, man, so tak' anither bite."

He managed to rouse from the tired slumber and, forcing a smile, swallowed another mouthful of the steaming macaroni and cheese I had been devouring so hungrily.

There followed a summer-long battle with pigweed, shepherd's purse, bindweed, plantain, dandelions and quack grass. He preferred to use a U-shaped Dutch shuffle-hoe, I wielded the regular blade and we hacked and chopped, heaping the refuse in a wheelbarrow trundled along each long row in turn. When we finished one patch it was on to the next. After that had been cleared and the greening spuds hilled, we walked wearily over to the third or fourth areas and, days later, returned to the first to weed all over again. He was considerate of my age, bidding me to abandon the hoe and go water the cow, tend the chickens, or run errands for my mother. In such pleasant ways I was spared the full brunt of the suffering toil he endured day after day. The rains came often enough for good growth and gave us rest breaks when other matters needed attention. Once on a cloudy mid-July morning as we started to take up the tools for another full day's work, my mother slyly hinted that the family diet had not enough variety. She dispatched us off to the river to catch fish.

"Go tae yon Cronquist pool, not too far awa'."

The eddy lay north of the pioneer Cronquist acres and their high tight fences which enclosed a notoriously cranky bull. We followed the line to the river bank and climbed down to the backwater where my father jointed up his greenheart rod brought from Scotland and played in three goldeyes. After thus making sure of a catch, he let me try the tackle and thereby committed me to a life-long addiction to angling.

"You might as well go ahead and clean them," he advised, nursing along his pipe. With the cleaned fish in the family haversack, the mile and a half walk home seemed pleasantly short. Our vacation interlude ended when we came in sight of the white-flowered potato patches, for we knew they needed more work.

He excused me from hoe duty several more times that summer and early autumn, sending me berrying. Saskatoons were plumply grape-sized that year, bursting with sweet juices. Picking berries provided me with shade from the sun, proximity to singing birds, gave me sightings of multi-hued butterflies and my first close look at a hummingbird hawk moth. I had glimpses of scolding red squirrels, wary coyotes, and loud whistling woodchucks. Once back home with laden cans and good mind pictures of what had been enjoyed, it was on with the routine of hoeing those endless rows of spuds.

All the arduous planting, weeding, hilling, re-weeding and cultivating were mere preliminary tests of endurance for the desperate harvest time from mid-September on. Dig deep with a four-tined fork, lift and shake, dig twice more for extras. Spread these to dry and shove the fork under the next hill. Our crop was exceptionally heavy, almost too much to gather in the scant weeks remaining of open weather. We would leave several rows of tubers exposed on their hills to air as we toiled along the straight lines. Half an hour later we went back to hand pick and dust, discarding any that were forked or misshapen. Prime ones were loaded into the wheelbarrow and trundled back to the house. There they were transferred to pails, carried indoors and down into the enlarged dug-out cellar. At first they were placed in the waiting bins carefully one at a time, but as the four big fields yielded load after load of the gleaming yellow-white prizes, we reserved only one cellar bin for other vegetables: carrots, beets, turnips, and parsnips. Bunches of onions and heads of cabbage were hung on nails from the overhead beams. No more fussy care for individual potatoes, we heaped them all over the dugout in helter-skelter piles that soon bulged the basement. When the cellar was jammed full to the trap door, then wooden and cardboard boxes, pails, wash boilers, anything that would hold potatoes was pressed into service in the back kitchen. Sheets, blankets, even our winter coats and newspapers were placed on top to keep the tubers warm and safe. On the last day of harvesting, there came a gasping sigh of relief from my father as he emptied the final pailful and collapsed into his chair where he fainted dead away with combined relief and exhaustion.

"Och, Willie," my mother crooned to him when our cold cloth applications had revived him. "Ye're not tae do this sort o' wurrrrk

anither year.'' When he nodded weakly, she became brisk of tone.
''Aye, it's back tae yer travels again come spring. It's a safer way
fer you to earrrn oor livin'. Fer noo, oor biggest worry is who'll
buy all this monster lot o' tatties?''

Ours had been virgin ground, never before sown to any domestic
plants. By some fluke potato crops in the town and district were either
scarce or hailed out, some being outright failures. Soon individuals,
storekeepers, even the usually self-sufficient farmers came seeking
the result of our summer's work. The asking price was 50¢ a bushel,
45¢ if the buyers supplied their own gunny sacks or empty box containers. By the time snow lay deeply around and winter had closed
in upon us, most of our treasure had been sold. Then our household
seemed secure against the vagaries of the foreseeable future.

Throughout the lean times from the March arrival day on the
acreage until after the harvest ended in early October, we had lived
frugally. We bought beef liver at 5¢ a pound and ate it often. A nickel
was charged for the big knuckled soup bones from which my mother
created savoury Scotch broth thick with swollen barley, nourishing
vegetables, and edible weeds. There were infrequent variations of
river fish, but too many meals of macaroni. We had lots of wild fruits
such as the plentiful saskatoons, wild raspberries, sour gooseberries
with only a hint of sweetening, and autumn's tart cranberries. Now
silver coins had been handed in and safely stored away, we were
treated to filling stews of round steak at 20¢ a pound, many a pot
roast, once the sheer luxury of a standing rib roast with rich brown
gravy. We were solvent once more and joyously grateful.

''Let's have a turkey, like we did in Calgary,'' Charlie teased
as Christmas drew near.

''Na, na—dinna be extravagant,'' my mother chided. I repeated
the long-syllabled word over and over, pleased with the elaborate
sound of it. ''Twill be one o' the hens. Wee laddie,'' she turned
to me, ''ye'll mind an' pick oot one that's no layin', then Charlie'll
do the rest.''

''W-e-l-l.''

''It's easy,'' Charlie told me. ''Go into the coop after dark and feel along the roosts. When you find a hen that hasn't an egg-swollen belly, grab her legs and stuff her into a brooder box until morning. She'll become our Christmas dinner.''

The night before Christmas Eve, I made my morose way into the coop which shared the warmth of the cow's body-heat from her nearby stall. Cautiously I fingered the undersides of poultry. The fourth bird stirred and wakened, whereupon my hand received a sharp rap as the rooster protested the indignity of having his bottom fondled. His shocked cackles roused the whole pen. The night's calm was raucously shattered with a bedlam of frantic clucks and next instant, a flurry of wings filled the cramped quarters. In the utter confusion that followed and half dazed by head buffetings, I glimpsed one stationary dim shape within easy reach and snatched it from the roost and thrust the squawking body into the waiting box.

Consternation! When Charlie performed the execution next morning, after the plucking he used a knife to explore inside the bird. As his red-stained hands drew out reeking stuff, we saw several partially formed eggs nestled within the once-productive fowl.

''Ye daft gommeral!'' my mother raged at me. ''We need every layer fer the lang cold months ahead. Ahhh,weel,'' she bestowed a forgiving pat on my shoulder. ''It's a sonsy fat one ye chose, and no doobt she'll mak' us a braw big dinner.''

She did.

Prairie and Postie

Mourning doves whooing overhead in Manitoba maples outside our home in Portage la Prairie aroused my curiosity as a two-year old. A year later on flat lands of a farm three miles from Esterhazy, Saskatchewan, several species which farmers called grass birds were numerous in variety and different in behavior. It was a bleak farm, the outlook barren of trees in all directions except for a small coulee at one edge. There we scrounged for firewood as winter approached and more birds were discovered. Thaddy, ten years my senior, encouraged me to make rough sketches of those that intrigued me, helping to add words of descriptive colours.

Before winter blizzards came, a rope was stretched between the house and cosy barn with its warm smelling cow. Neighbouring farmers had advised us that such a rope was essential as a winter-long hand guideline to prevent us from getting lost. During raging white-out storms, four steps away from the stove-heated house both it and the barn were completely blocked from sight by swirling snows. The rope remained our only thread of reality in the wild space between the buildings. Time hung heavy indoors on savage days, whereupon Thaddy decided to teach his little brother to read from one of the few books available, our mother's Bible.

"Let not your heart be troubled: ye believe in God, believe

also in me. In my Father's house are many mansions. If it were not so, I would have told you. I go to prepare a place for you.''

It became a memory test for my young brain. The finished sequence was chanted in a sing-song to cement the words in my mind. It was not until many years later, at the time of Thaddy's death in the 1918 flu, that I learned this passage was part of the funeral oration.

Perhaps it was my chanting performance that encouraged him to seek out another much slimmer volume, a collection of Scottish songs. These added immensely to the pleasure of reading. Not only were meanings clearer to me, but my mother was prompted by our practices to set aside her mending and get out her mandolin. She played the tunes and sang the cheery melodies, our young voices joining hers in familiar choruses.

Eventually frigid winter's hold loosened on the land; green grass and tiny pale leaves appeared again. With the new learning, I put more details on sketches of returning migrants. All of us were fascinated when birds our neighbours called prairie chickens congregated on a knoll near the coulee to strut, wing-drag, and boom out amazing sounds. Their abandoned behaviour at this season was markedly different from 'tuk-tuk-tukka-tuk' alarm chirps of the previous autumn, or anytime we happened to flush a flock of the sharp-tailed grouse on the sunnier days of winter when we walked for exercise or collected firewood. My previous sketches looked childish to my four-year-old eyes; many were re-drawn with Thaddy's helpful descriptions. We even tried to translate whistles of birds into word sounds. The new sketches were carefully stored among my treasures, older ones discarded only when ''that bird'' had been seen again and described more carefully.

''Boys, gather aroon','' my mother announced one day. ''We're tae gang oot tae a city called Calgary, where yer fayther's wurrrk has taken him. All o' ye pitch in and help me pack.''

''Will we pack Bishop, too?''

A grim line settled across my mother's mouth and she shook her head. Later I learned that another farm family was to have our black collie. How his tail wagged in response to my tearful hugs on our last day at the farm!

Hillhurst, then Mewata Park districts were our first Calgary locations, but life became marvelous for me when we moved to an avenue just south of Prince's Island on the Bow River. A narrow foot-bridge led across to the well wooded paradise where we three brothers spent much of our spare time. The lower end was occupied by a lumber company and a gruff-voiced workman warned us to stay away from there. Back upstream again, a movement near the top of a cottonwood tree caught my attention.

"Look, it's orange and black." The bird was not shy as it uttered a strong sounding warble.

"Here's my pad," my brother offered. A St. Vitus dance illness in Scotland had weakened his vision and Thaddy used oil paintings as a form of therapy. He always carried a small pad on our outings in hopes of viewing a scene that could later be reproduced in colors. "Make good notes this time, because he looks a special member of our sanctuary." It was the first time I remembered hearing and understanding what was meant by 'sanctuary'; Prince's Island became our first. Thaddy added: "I forgot to look for a bird book when I was at the library the other night."

This casually dropped information caught my attention. Next day was Saturday with no school. Whatever house chores were mine that morning were hurried through, lunch bolted, then my collection of sketches from Esterhazy and recent island discoveries were placed in a scribbler for protection. I went eagerly over to the sandstone library building set in the midst of lawns, flower beds, and soldiers-on-horseback statues of Central Park. One of the staff ladies noticed me and offered to help. She laughed when she first glanced at the pages, but became serious as she fathomed the reason for the amateurish sketches. In another moment two other ladies joined her behind the desk and they regarded me kindly as my queries poured out about learning the names of birds.

"Yes, of course we have bird books," the first lady said. Soon these were spread out for my examination. From that moment on, librarians became my friends.

Yet life in Calgary was not confined to enjoyment on Prince's Island and visiting the lady informants at Central Park. Jackie had become my chum; he lived back of a corner grocery store his father owned. My mother liked to shop there, and with her one time I noticed a peculiar odour from a brown mixture in an open barrel.

"It's something new called peanut butter," Jackie told me. "It's no good if you eat it by itself, but it's nice spread on crackers."

One snowy Christmas Eve when I got home from the library my mother said Jackie wanted me.

"He's doon under the street light at Mrs. Brown's corner, and he wants ye tae hurry. He said it wis important."

Off I ran to join Jackie, who greeted me with alarming news.

"It's Postie. He's behind the hedge, and he can't walk."

We two seven-year-olds stared down at roly-poly Postie, who beamed up at us from a snow drift and said:

"Comes only once a year...Chrisssmusss Eve! Merry Chrissmussss."

Jackie and I realized at once that we had a crisis on our hands.

"We'll have to deliver the letters," Jackie decided. "You can read, so you sort them and I'll carry 'em in."

Somehow we got the heavy man onto Jackie's flat hand-sled. Postie was happy as we began our ordeal. When he slid off, the accident evoked hilarious glee from him, but it strained us to get him loaded again. At last we found an empty cardboard box which had fallen off a dray. We crowded him into it, his mail bag perched on top of his ample stomach. The packet of letters for our avenue was on top and I sorted, then Jackie delivered them to the homes. Mrs. Anderson was out on her porch to receive hers and declared it was a disgrace. Jackie wondered what she meant. I did not know nor care, for between the business of sorting the mail and keeping Postie quiet, I was busy. Postie wanted to sing a Christmas carol, whereupon the raucous loudness of his untamed tenor alarmed us.

"Shhhhhh, Postie."

"Why sssshhhhhhh? It's Chrisssmusss Evvveeee. Yipppeeeee!"

"Sing him your flow song," Jackie suggested. "Maybe it'll

quiet him down. Who's next?''

After he had letters for another house, I tried to interest Postie in Flow Gently, Sweet Afton. He would have none of it.

"Sing the cranky ssssongggg," Postie ordered.

The cranky song? Jackie and I dragged the sled to our next stop. As I peered at another handful of letters Jackie had an inspiration.

"He means the loony song."

"Ohhh, that one. Listen, Postie: 'I, like a great big muckle loon, Upon a thistle I sat doon; I nearly jumped up tae the moon, On the braes of Killie-crankie'."

Postie liked it. We continued to haul him and the Royal Mail along the three blocks, not without many tumbling episodes and loading struggles that taxed our small muscles. Yet we managed to coax the heavy man back into the box time after time and made sure no mail spilled from the all-important bag. Every letter intended for our section was sorted and delivered, thanks to fast-running Jackie, thanks to me soothing down the exuberant Postie with yet another verse of the cranky song.

" 'Toora-loora-loora-loo, They're needing monkeys in the zoo; Ye better gang awa' the noo, A-fore they come and tak' you'."

We were exhausted when we met Mr. Bob standing under a lamp post. He was the beat policeman.

"Just a minute, boys," Mr. Bob spoke sharply, stepping over to peer down at the recumbent form of Postie, who looked up at him solemnly.

"Merry Chrisssmusssss, Robert."

"Thomas! Oh, Thomas!" growled Mr. Bob. He asked what had happened, enquired if we were sure all the mail had been tended to properly, then nodded without his usual smile. "Very well, boys, I'll take over now. But you're not to say a word, understand? Not a word. Ahh—whose sleigh is this?... Jackie, I'll leave it at your back door after I finish with Postie. Hurry home, or you'll be late for supper. But remember, not a word."

Jackie and I were tired, our small frames aching after the strenuous exertions of the long haul down the avenue. Inner parts of our mittened hands were chafed sore from straining against the sled rope, while the inside of my wool tuque was wet with sweat. Worst of all, we were suddenly in despair after all the excitement of helping Postie. Neither of us had minded helping him, except....

"Mr. Bob sounded mad, didn't he?" Jackie phrased our mutual apprehension.

"Yes. What did he mean when he said 'not a word'? Did we do something wrong?"

"I don't know. Up 'til now, Mr. Bob's always been nice. But tonight, he sounded real angry."

"At us, too."

"Yes, at us. I wonder why?"

We lapsed into silence, a silence broken by loud barking as half the neighbourhood dogs galloped into view. In front of them hopped a frantic rabbit.

"Save it!" shouted Jackie.

We flung ourselves in front of the pack, calling dogs by name. In the resulting chaos they tripped over us, yelping in frustration as the bunny scuttled into the screen of river bank trees and disappeared. The animals knew us and there were no bites that mattered. We patted them generously after we were upright again, getting whines of pleasure from them as we scratched behind their ears.

"I'm hungry," said Jackie. "Bye."

At home, inside the kitchen door, the family circle closed quickly around me. My mother's hand began to rise as though to strike, but my father spoke a restraining word. Thaddy and Charlie stared at me.

"Ye're late," my mother frowned. "Mrs. Anderson wis here, verra angry. What do ye have tae say fer yersel'?"

"Jackie needed help to deliver the mail. Here's ours."

She took the letters, eyes widening with pleasure as she saw Scottish stamps on them. But she quickly turned back to me with another scowl. I saw my father's shoulders twitching and knew he was shaking with controlled laughter. His three sons looked at him in puzzlement. What was there to laugh about at that moment?

"Never mind, Liz. Serve up supper and leave him alone. He

doesn't know."

"What don't I know?" I fiercely demanded.

At this arrogant question, my mother broke into laughter that became almost hysterical. Subsiding at last, she tugged my ear fondly and gave her answer.

"Ye dinna ken a lot o' things, wee laddie. Which is mayhap just as weel. Noo, get oot o' yer outer clothes and wash up for supper."

• • •

Through the intervening years there have been many happy times of family fun at the Christmas season. There was one year when the children seemed especially joyous as Marjorie and I joined their fun in making a huge snowman on the front lawn. Another time Heather and Greg excavated a large drift in the yard where they crawled in and out in daring sub-polar worlds of adventure. Wet mittens, soggy tuques and nippy noses were of little concern. Sleigh rides, moonlit walks in the sparkling wonderlands of winter, and the fascinating pastime of unravelling wild tracks have given us merry thoughts and shared laughter to cherish.

First frost visited our home area in 1985 on the night of September 17, late for our district. Only two days earlier we had walked around the meadow entranced by scarlet leaves of Ginneli maples, gold of pincherries high-lighted against greens of aspen poplars, osier dogwoods had purple tinges, while at the wild edge the leaves of roses shone like small red torches. After we returned from a town shopping trip, we noticed that wind had stripped off most of the vivid maple leaves. However, other contrasts were still there, beautiful colors we enjoyed from every house window.

Then the white birch tree close to the front yard came alive with movement. It was full of migrants. Myrtle, Canada, and yellow warblers, kinglets, juncoes, and pine siskins, the latter species arriving to spend the winter season with us. As we stood watching, a pileated woodpecker flew over and did not heed the chunk of suet on which a downy was feeding. Red-tailed hawks soared by, flocks of noisy crows blackened the far tree tops, and there was a clustered flock of nine mallards off on the horizon. The radio announcer's forecast of rain proved false, because after sundown the wind-swept sky blazed with stars. When we stepped outside to get a wider view of them, our breath puffed out in steaming vapour.

"This time it'll freeze," Marjorie predicted.

"Yes, but it's been a grand autumn."

"I'm not complaining."

The chill had been anticipated; tomatoes, squash, peas and beans had been harvested. On the morning of the 18th, Marjorie joined me outdoors to pull haulms of vegetables that would grow no more this season. We took down screens that had held up peavines, removed support laths from withered flowers, bundled together marking sticks which had dotted the planted rows. As the cold seeped into us, we decided on the extra precaution of digging the potatoes. These were of the Norland variety, a bright pink and smooth-skinned crop looking handsome against the dark soil. After they had been stored indoors, one other chore remained.

"Shall I walk out for the mail before lunch?" I asked.

"You must be cold, like me. Let's spoil ourselves and let the car go the half-mile and back."

We agreed to be spoiled, this once.

The Musicians

My mother's mandolin had four silken ribbons of Black Watch tartan slung from a cord hooked at the neck. When she drew the instrument out of the faded humpbacked case, the ribbons swirled with a flourish on that early winter day. My father put down the book he had been reading and reached for his violin. By the look of it, this was to be a concert and I squirmed contentedly into a corner of the couch and prepared to watch and listen.

"We could try Afton Water," she suggested.

"That will be fine," agreed my father, and made raspy scraping sounds on the violin as she tinkled the A-string to help him with the tuning. While this tedious process was going on, I stared again at the graceful contour of the round-backed mandolin. Its polished yellow bowl was rimmed with black lines where the panels of wood were joined together, the front opening decorated with handsome brown patterns, the ebony fingering board divided by brassy frets. A beautiful instrument, much loved by our family. As my father was still twisting on a peg and plucking the second string of tuning, it seemed an appropriate time to enquire about the history of the mandolin.

"It came from Glasgow," she replied. "Years back noo, aroon' 1892 when I wis a young wummon o' twenty."

1892 seemed ages ago, because I was a product of another century.

"Was it made in Glasgow?"

"I dinna ken aboot that. There were craft folk in Scotland who made music-makkin' things, but I never found a maker's name on it."

My father raised his eyes from his instrument, momentarily forgetting the tuning as he became aware of our discussion.

"Italy," he said, and bent again to his task.

"Whit aboot Italy?"

"It was made in Italy," he answered as he tackled the third string.

"I'm no' sure," my mother deliberated. "I mind it wis given to me by my music-teacher, but dear knows whaur he got it, Italy or Spain or Glasgow itself."

My father scowled, shaking his head in contradiction. He said that, yes, her music-teacher had given her the first mandolin, but this was a different one.

"I gave it to you myself, and it was made in Italy. The man at the music shop told me that."

"Away with ye, man," she protested. "My music-teacher gi'ed me this one."

"No, you gave that first one to your sister, after I presented you with this much better instrument."

"I'm thinkin' it was the ither way," my mother said with some asperity. "When we married an' had our first twa bairns and decided to leave the Auld Countree, that's when I gave yours tae my sister and I brought this one alang tae North Americky."

"The one I chose you're holding now," my father was emphatic. He laid his violin on the kitchen table and began pacing the room in exasperation. "I remember that I had to save up for months, because I had my eye on the best mandolin in the store. That one. You took the tartan ribbons off your first one and tied them on this when we agreed to sail—likely that's where you became confused about which was which. You were fond of the ribbons, and they're still a fine ornamental touch."

She stroked a melancholy chord on the mandolin under discussion and dropped the pick hand to her lap.

"Willie, d'ye not think I'd ken my ain instryment? I tell ye, man, this is the verra same my teacher gi'ed me."

"No, Liz. I recall how pleased you were when I handed that one to you. It's got a fine mellow tone."

"Fiddle-da-dee aboot the tone!" she was really agitated now. "Willie, it's the mandolin we're talkin' aboot. My teacher..."

"But wife, he gave you the smaller one, the mandolin you learned on and left in Scotland. This is the Italian model I bought you, my best courting gift."

His beard quivered with rising emotion and they exchanged glances that added sparks to the feud. I slipped off the couch and went along the hall to my narrow bedroom and got out my whistle. This was a tinny thing with holes punched at intervals along the stalk, bought after much thought from Eaton's. It had cost me 15 cents; I had earned the money by cleaning one neighbour's chicken coop and thinning turnips for another. There had been a long debate within myself about the assorted merits of catalogue offerings, because there was a mysterious article called an ocarina which sorely tempted me. Getting it would have meant spending a nickel more than my entire capital at the time. Finally the whistle had been chosen when the family order was mailed in. The remaining 20 cents of my hoard was saved for the emergency needs of boyhood.

I went over to the window with my whistle, blew into it softly, and began with slow deliberation to finger "God Save the King." There were some major mistakes, such as when I blew too forcefully a high note and the squeak jumped a whole octave and hurt my ears. I started all over again, more surely and solemnly this time after the first run. I was just "sending him victorious" when footsteps sounded in the hall and my mother's head poked around the door frame.

"Dinna treat King Geordie like that, laddie. Try 'Hame Sweet Hame' and give the King a wee holiday."

"But I only know 'God Save the King'," I said.

"Then 'tis time ye learnt anither piece. That song ye're learnin' at school called Polly Wolly Doodle—try it."

"It's too fast for me. Are you having a concert?"

"Aye, yer fayther's finished his tuning, and he's just beginnin' 'The Wee Cooper o' Fife'."

I scooted back to my corner of the couch and soon the lilting melody of that old nonsense song filled the kitchen.

" 'Nickety-nackety-noo-noo-noo'," my mother sang, and I joined in the chorus part: " 'Hi wulla-wullicka-Ho John Dougal alang-kwa rooshety roo-roo-roo'."

The two instruments blended well. Next we had 'Highland Laddie', then my favorite 'Afton Water'.

I smiled at the way my father's brown beard stuck out on the violin's chin-rest, and although he was much too self-contained to drop his fiddle and join the singing, his eyes glowed with the family fun and relish of the old tunes. At length my mother, gasping for breath, reached for the mandolin case.

"Yer fayther needs tae get back to his readin', and I'm going tae mak' some parkins."

"Good!" Parkin cookies were full of oatmeal and molasses, crunchy treats we all liked. "Do you need help, mixing the spices?"

"I'll manage," she said, though normally she welcomed help with such things because the spice scent bothered her asthma. "If ye dinna wish tae use yer whustle anymore, gang oot and look at yer birds."

Which meant I was free to do anything I chose on that Saturday afternoon with chores finished. So I trotted cheerfully outside to decide on the prospect of either going into the nearby spruce woods to follow tracks in the snow, or walking along the road into the farther adventures of Cruickshank's farm where I had sighted a flock of white-winged crossbills the week before. My father raised his eyes from his book to give me a slightly abstracted nod as I left the kitchen, while my mother was busily rolling up her sleeves and delving into the flour bin.

Actually, I was distracted on the way to the farm by the jerky spoor of a hunting weasel. As I followed the twin-dotted tracks from mouse-hole to hole, I thought of the musical abilities of our family members. My mother was without question the most talented, able to play any tune she happened to hear and put in chord trills and tremolo runs. She had a great trove of melodic memories, mostly old Scottish ballads and popular hits of the American scene learned during their stay in New York City.

"German bands cam' aroon' the street corners every few days. They knew a' the new pieces in favour, as well as their ain music frae over the watters, but I got awfu' fed up wi' their Atch-der-loober-August something. A song called 'East Side, West Side' was the rage, back then."

My father tried out his violin every third or fourth weekend, when home from his travels. He had once told me that he had been adept on it, but quickly amended this modest boast with the qualification that, with a violin, a person had to practice daily to become bearable to listeners. When we first came to Red Deer city in the spring of 1918, I had wanted him to teach me how to play the fiddle. Thaddy had offered to endure my learning period and teach me to read music. My father vetoed the idea, counselling that I should take up the flute instead.

"A flute has a soothing tone. You'd drive us mad with violin squawks, better wait and learn the flute."

During the interval since there had been the devastating Spanish Influenza epidemic, Thaddy had died of it last December, and we had moved to this acreage a mile from town. My brother Charlie, seven years my senior, was an expert on the mouth-organ and sometimes he and my mother played duets together.

Charlie was extremely versatile. His next musical achievement required the acquisition of an empty five-gallon tin, an old broom handle, a spare violin peg, a fret-sawed bridge, a length of gut string borrowed from our friend Waldo's cello, and the use of my father's violin bow. When he drew that freshly rosined bow across the tautly stretched gut, a screaming wail came from deep inside the anguished soul of the large tin can. Nobby, our Airedale dog after whom I'd received my nickname, reared back on his tan haunches and let heaven know that all hell had broken loose down here below.

"Wheest! Wheest:" cried my mother, rushing from the house.

Fortunately she did not know of my silent imaginings of Nobby's howled comment, else I would have been soundly cuffed on both ears, had my tongue lathered with soap, and sent to bed without supper. Charlie and I moved, after putting Nobby into Bessie's stable and snibbing the door shut, over to the edge of the woodland path in front of the empty cabin that was later to become my home. There my brother fingered the broom handle and sawed resolutely away on the monster mock fiddle, and siren-like moans screeched from the dark interior of the erstwhile oil drum.

"Wonderful!" announced Charlie.

I said nothing at all.

"It sounds pretty good, doesn't it?" he prompted.

"Your mouth-organ playing is a lot better."

"Oh, but I'm just learning how to master this. In a month's time it'll boom out as good as Waldo's bass cello."

In point of fact, in a month's time Charlie had swapped the five-gallon groaner for an assortment of old tools, which he sharpened, plus a handful of .22 rifle shells. From some other source he had previously obtained a single-shot .22 rifle. With the aid of the cartridges, Charlie practiced back of the barn on a ringed bull's eye. After six shots, he was satisfied that he could keep the family supplied with rabbits and partridges, come autumn.

He became even more accomplished on the mouth-organ, my father's already humble prowess on the violin diminished through lack of playing, while my mother's nimble fingers coaxed all sorts of musical goodies from the mellow-toned mandolin. I never acquired a flute, the 15-cent tin whistle being the nearest substitute. I made it wander through the halls of 'Home Sweet Home' and, later after meeting Marjorie, I practised but did not perfect 'Believe Me If All Those Endearing Young Charms.' I played the number with quavering passion one evening when she was visiting at our home.

"Believe me, Romeo, I nearly gave up on you then and there," Marjorie told me much later after our union was a minister-blessed fact. "It's a lucky thing your mother made tea to divert you from the shrilling pathos of that tin whistle. Mind you, I did consider the sentiment—or was it sediment?—involved. By the way, whatever happened to that whistle?''

    ''It's in my bottom drawer, good as ever.''

    She looked skeptical, and murmured:

    ''It was never 'good'.''

Young Miss Marshall

While our Wood family was having its adventures, Marjorie came with her mother and three older brothers from Sault Ste. Marie on the long, slow train journey westward to Calgary, switched to another train and moved northward. First to Kathyrn, a prairie farm, then on to Iowalta not far from Lacombe. Mrs. Marshall's father had bought the quarter-section farms at these two locations during the boom year of 1910.

The lady decided the scenery around Iowalta was more to her liking than the flat prairie country at Kathyrn, so she engaged the Taylor family to build a small house and barn on the property. While waiting for its completion, mother and family stayed temporarily in a one-roomed log cabin. Its chief memorable feature being 11 large, but fortunately deserted, yellow-jacket wasps' nests spaced closely along the roof beams. They were in their new farm home on Marjorie's birthday on November 11th when young Strawsie Taylor of the carpenter family came galloping around the neighbourhood on horseback shouting an important message.

"Armistice! Armistice! There is Peace!"

The 1914-1918 war had just ended on the 11th hour of the 11th day of the 11th month.

Marjorie's character showed early signs of her future depend-

ability at Iowalta. She rode a horse named Buster to school, and also rode the same fat animal to round up the cows every evening, singing happily all the while. One particular time after she got down to close the pasture gate, when she climbed the boards to re-mount the horse, Buster refused to turn sideways and kept his nose towards her. Patiently she re-led the horse back broadside to the gate, but by the time she had climbed up high enough to mount, wily old Buster had eased himself away out at the bridle's length beyond reach. After the fifth failure, Marjorie set her mouth and led the horse homeward on foot. However, she took care to shoo all the cows ahead of her. Her mother listened to the reason for the delay, smiled and said:

"You'll do!"

A year later Mrs. Marshall decided she needed more land for a family of four and sold the Iowalta property to finance the down payment on a section of land alongside the Red Deer River. The new location, with only half of its wide acres broken to cultivation, was situated at the dead end of a road in an isolated tangle of beautiful landscape known locally as "The Jungles." It was 24 miles southeast of Lacombe, their major shopping town at the time as there was no near bridge across the river to provide access to Red Deer. The hamlet of Joffre, seven miles away, had a general store to serve the district, also a grain elevator as a flag stop on the C.N. Railway at this point. The Jungles farm became Marjorie's childhood home remembered so fondly through the mist of years. The C.P. Brocks were their closest neighbours to the west. Tom and Dorothy Brock being near enough to Jim and Marjorie's ages to become their good companions.

"There were marked differences between our two groups of brothers and sisters. The Brock kids impressed us at the time because they were allowed to swear, strictly forbidden to us. We made up for this lack in our ability to light fires, a trait they greatly envied. My Mother and Dad had once been leaders of a Boy Scout troop in the Dakotas, so Mother taught us all the safety rules regarding matches and campfires. If Jim and I got a couple of matches from home and chose sites among the river shore gravels or sand bars, promising always to put the flames out afterward, we were sure of attracting the admiration of Tom and Dorothy Brock. Their family home had gone up in smoke, reason enough for them all to be cautious of fire. So they were pleased whenever Jim or I announced we would light a campfire down on the river bank. On such occasions we would raid the two family coops for extra eggs, get slices of bread and butter from our mothers, and rapturously set off for a picnic to hard-boil the eggs. We had our little feasts there all through the summer. I remember gulls swooping in close to see if we would spare them any crumbs.''

Under Jim's guidance, the four became known as the Appy Gang. C-appy, H-appy, T-appy, and S-appy; Marjorie refuses to recall which one was Sappy. Other youngsters of the neighbourhood clamoured to join in and rode seven or eight miles and more for the weekly outings. Official meetings were held near a cave known as the Porcupine Den, a narrow hollow under a sandstone rock in which the young Marshalls had found some quills. These playmates attended Brookfield School, four and a half miles from Marjorie's home. Jim and Marjorie rode horseback daily throughout the school year, carrying lunches for the one-hour noon break then allowed at rural classrooms. Jim was mounted on the faster horse and often arrived home long before his little sister. Indeed, Marjorie liked to dally on the homeward road singing at the top of her lungs while her elderly steed sauntered along at its own leisurely pace.

"I call that pair 'Thunder and Lightning'," one farmer joked, referring to Marjorie's boisterous singing and the animal's lack of speed.

• • •

Isaac Low, an Englishman who had settled earlier on land farther downstream, liked to take a shortcut to Joffre store through the Marshall farmyard and in this way became a friend and neighbour. He was always willing to do little shopping errands or act as mailman. "Ike" as he was affectionately called, was once digging himself a new well when another neighbour arrived to say he would like to buy some land.

Mr. Low owned a parcel at some distance from his riverbank holdings. At the moment Ike was eight feet down the hole, but instead of climbing the ladder and coming out for a discussion, he said:

"The title's at the left in the top drawer of my bureau. Go get it, look it over, and make me an offer."

A price was mutually agreed upon in a few give-and-take exchanges. The papers were dropped down for Mr. Low to sign a transfer of ownership, sent back up in a bucket. The cash was put in the bureau drawer to await Ike's attention later.

"Now we've finished our business," the buyer said, "I'll shed my jacket and give you a hand with this well."

The simple transaction involving nearly a thousand dollars gives an idea of the lifelong respect and trust between pioneer neighbours.

Marjorie remembers that Mr. Low lost three pigs in separate raids of a marauding black bear. Little-Son-of-Annoss, a well known Cree hunter, was summoned to dispatch the offending animal. But when the Indian rode to Ike's place, he had other ideas than waiting in ambush for the next raid of the prowling bear.

"I go get married today, too busy to hunt. For one dollar I sell you a bear-killing shell."

Dubiously Ike parted with the money and examined his purchase. The .12-gauge shotgun shell had been opened, wads removed and more black powder added, the bird-shot all being firmly cemented together with candle wax before the outer wads had been crudely replaced. Mr. Low was not convinced it was a worthwhile bargain, yet he loaded it into one chamber of his double-barrelled gun and set the weapon handy to his door. A day or so later his dog treed the bear behind the pigpen. Alerted by the furious barking, Ike got the gun and ran toward the noisy scene. Out of breath, he rounded the corner of the pigpen and found himself a scant 15 feet from the angry bear halfway up a small poplar. Greatly daring, the man aimed at the bear's midriff and pulled the trigger. The terrific recoil of the over-charged shell sent him sprawling backwards with an aching shoulder. When Ike sat up and stared around, the bear was stretched dead on the ground near his feet and his hound was worrying the animal's neck fur and

wagging its tail in full approval of his master's skill.

Two weeks later Little-Son came again.

"I hear about battle. You owe me a dollar more, because you killed the bear with my good medicine shell."

Mr. Low judged that the bridegroom needed a present. He gave him a slab of bacon, two loaves of bread, half a pound of tea and a free lunch but no dollar. They parted the best of friends.

• • •

One Sunday morning Mrs. Marshall took Marjorie with her in a two-seater cart with the mare, Cyclone, hitched between the shafts. They were church bound, the service to be held in the Brookfield school where a missionary preacher came once a month to conduct services. A couple of miles from home the mare spied a large roadside pond and began to wade in to get a drink. However, the bank sloped off sharply and the surprised Cyclone slid down and into the deep water. Plunging across the pool, hooking its head over the barbed-wire fence's top strand, the mare stayed there and resolutely refused to obey reins or urgent commands. Marjorie, aged 12 at the time, jumped over-board and dog-paddled back to the road.

"I was held up like a cork by the spreading folds of my coat. It was just like wearing a pair of water-wings."

Once on dry land again, she was dismayed to see that her mother had not followed her example. Mrs. Marshall was still stranded atop the cart seat out in the pond. Casting off the soaked and heavy coat, Marjorie cried:

"I'll save you, Mother! I'll save you!"

She was about to jump in for the return swim when her mother shouted one word.

"STOP!"

The whiplash tone of voice halted young Miss Marshall in her tracks. The lady calmly proceeded to instruct her daughter to go to the nearest clump of bush and find a long pole. This was brought back and stretched out towards the mother, who grasped it firmly, then stepped off the cart into water up to her neck and waded ashore. Next, Marjorie ran to the nearest farm to get help to rescue horse and cart.

"The two men got soaked doing it, but eventually they managed to lead Cyclone and cart to safety. First, though, they drove us to the farmhouse to dry out. We didn't try to keep our church attendance record straight for that day. For a short while, some of our friends teased Mother about 'Mrs. Marshall's Annual Bath.' I think Mother didn't appreciate the joke."

Mrs. Marshall unwittingly spoiled Marjorie's early fondness for cottage cheese. One spring day after making a fresh batch, instead of leaving it in the colander to drain, the resourceful lady hung the bag out on the clothesline to drip. Polly, one of their cows and an expert at getting through fences, spied the juicy-looking cotton bag oozing white drops. She dispensed with the barrier in short order and was soon sucking blissfully on the cottage cheese. Marjorie looked out the window just in time to see the middle of this performance. From then on, she would not touch another spoonful of the homemade article.

She laughed as she recalled the memory of Polly at the bag and remembered another dietary problem.

"I've told you about the hard-boiled egg picnics we had with the Brocks. Well, once a faithless biddy of a broody hen gave up setting on a batch of eggs she'd hidden away in some buck brush, back of the barn. One of our sheep chanced to trample the nest a month later and I heard it give a choking gasp. When I investigated, the air all around those rotten eggs was ghastly and putrid. Since minding the hens was my job, I had to find a spade and bury the mess. For a long spell afterwards, I wasn't very keen on eating eggs."

The two older brothers having returned to the States to attend college, Mrs. Marshall engaged her first hired man to help with the rougher chores of farming. The new-comer from London, England, serenaded them with popular verses from 'The Mikado' comic opera. After he had sung them a solo, he paused and looked at them with a serious expression.

"You can't hear it, I suppose? While I'm singing, in my head there's a whole orchestra and chorus off behind me producing all the proper accompaniments at exactly the right time. To me, it sounds perfectly wonderful!''

Marjorie decided to take part in the next school fair. She rehearsed the story of Madeleine de Verchères, the young 14-year-old who defended her father's fort until an army arrived to relieve the siege. Mrs. Marshall had Marjorie go to the top of a nearby hill, turn and face her, then tell the story clearly and distinctly so that a large grandstand audience could hear every word. When the day of competition arrived, Marjorie dressed in an old black petticoat of her mother, a period white blouse, and put on an extra auburn ''switch'' to make her own short hair look more typical of the bygone time. Needless to add, she won first prize for rural scholars at Red Deer in front of an enthusiastic crowd. On the drive home she was rather subdued in her joy regarding the victory; the prize awarded was a picture of La Vérendrye viewing the Rockies. She had hoped for something a little more useful.

Marjorie's mother had a great deal of ability and soon shared her talents with her neighbours. Organizing a community club, she made sure that farm wives had an opportunity to broaden their horizons, to get away from their homes regularly for fellowship and relaxation. She also helped teachers to present plays and music for their annual Christmas concerts. Whenever a party was held at her home, there was certain to be a selection or two of worthwhile music as an addition to dance records.

• • •

When our star was in her mid-teens, the Marshall family moved into Red Deer after renting the farm to their Brock neighbours. The purpose of the move was two-fold. To let Jim and Marjorie attend high school after the grade nine limitations of the rural school room; secondly, to give Mrs. Marshall a chance to indulge in her life-long ambition to operate a gift shop. When the shop opened her artistic training at Chicago's Art Institute gave a basis for much expression of her various skills. She had prepared an amazing assortment of exquisitely hand-crafted articles for sale, among them: leather purses with burnt designs on their sides and handles, trays and bowls hammered out of brass and copper sheets, brightly coloured woodwork presented as small shelves and brackets, original painted patterns on scarves and shawls, and stacks of fancy cushions stuffed with her own farm's sheep wool. Unhappily, the Depression of the Dirty Thirties had a strangle-hold on the region at the time. The shop barely earned them a living, never receiving the wider response she had expected. Soon she had to turn to private nursing to make ends meet.

Marjorie very much enjoyed town life. She joined the high school Fliers basketball team and became goalie of the ladies Amazon Hockey Club, helping both teams to win provincial championships that winter. She also attended Girl Guide activities and sang in a church choir, and became an active member of many of the town's clubs of young people and made many friends. When the five-year lease was up on the farm, Marjorie was loath to return to the isolated country home. Soon she obtained work and was back in Red Deer.

I had first seen her as a girl of 11 and noted the sparkling beauty of her dark eyes. When she blossomed into an extremely attractive young lady at Red Deer, we met again and mutually agreed to "go steady." After what seemed to us a very long engagement, our marriage took place on a bitterly cold February day in 1936. As we travelled by train to start our honeymoon holiday, I went along the coach to buy a newspaper. The conductor tapped me on the shoulder.

"Your wife tells me you have the tickets."

Startled, I demanded:

"My what?"

As he accepted the quickly produced tickets and my apology, the conductor's smile was kind and fatherly.

"Good luck," he murmured.

We feel that we have been blessed with it, ever since.

Diamonds

One dark night when my chum Sid Snell was driving us southward past the east end of Hazlett's Slough, we slowed and rolled down the windows to listen for night calls of water birds.

"Stop!" I yelled. "Jewels beyond your headlights."

Scores of white, diamond-like pin points flashed at us from the road.

"They're moving," Sid said as he applied brakes. "Let's go have a look."

We walked forward, many of the shiny winkers going blank as our shadows loomed between them and the car. But in the fringes where the headlights still shone there were sparklers enough to lure us closer.

"I'll bet I know," my friend remarked. "It'll be a mass toad migration; I've heard about them."

When we reached the nearest creatures the mystery was solved. They were northern tiger salamanders, their miniature dragon-like bodies scurrying noiselessly ahead of us as we approached. Sid returned to the car and eased it forward to bring the herd into sharper focus. There were about a hundred of them and I picked up one, holding it carefully to avoid squeezing the soft body. It was a muddy brown with darker stripes, about seven inches long from its blunt snout to the end of the tapering tail. While it squirmed at first, soon it sat quietly

on my palm and peered up at the reflection of my glasses.

At that moment we heard the hum of another car and looked back to see the lights of it not far to the north.

"Sid, we've got to stop it or these things will get run over."

"I'll get the flashlight and flag it down. You start shooing salamanders off the road."

The season was early May, the pond period for toads was over and likely the same nature rule held true for other amphibians. As the sound of the approaching car grew in volume, I broke off a willow branch from a roadside shrub and used the leafy plume as a broom to hurry the exodus of the small crawlers. Sid halted the car and I heard a question and my friend's reassuring answer. A man came out as a woman's voice shrilled a protest.

"You're not going to go look at them, are you?"

"Sure I am. He says there's a hundred."

Sid and the man came into the doubled glow of the two sets of headlights as I picked up another protesting salamander to show the new-comer.

"Do they bite?"

"Oh, no," Sid laughed. "What a throng. Normally, we'd be lucky to see three or four in a whole summer."

"We find them under rhubarb leaves in gardens," I added. "Tonight we've chanced on a sudden migration from the big slough over there. When we first came along, the way their eyes shone I thought a load of jewels had spilled onto the hard top."

The man tentatively touched the salamander I held and exclaimed that its skin felt smoothly dry.

"I thought it'd be slimy," he confessed. "It's not ugly, either. I wonder if my wife'd care to see?"

He went back to consult her, while Sid hurriedly picked his way through the scurriers to pump his flashlight up and down to halt an oncoming car from the south. The extent of the migration mass measured 40 feet across, with more crawling out of the dew-wet grass on the slough side of the road. Perhaps there were 70 in sight by this time; we had estimated over a hundred at first and had no way of knowing how many had passed before we arrived. Their numbers were thinning out a few minutes later when five cars had been halted on either side of the migration route. All the men were interested, while three ladies joined the group and one scolded me for being too brisk with the willow branch broom.

"Don't hurt any," this motherly type admonished.

A younger lady wondered if a salamander would make an interesting house pet. Her male companion told her not to be ridiculous; abashed by the public rebuke, she returned to their car. The third lady,daringly, reached down and gingerly stroked one salamander's back with a timid forefinger. The motherly sort asked how it felt.

"Like a silk glove."

"That's nice."

We stood clustered on that warm night with a hint of rain above in the low clouds, the bossy cluck of coots not far away, while from the hills beyond Bill Hazlett's house El Coyote raised his rallying call. Once a nighthawk zoomed close overhead and a snipe whickered, but most of our attention was focused directly on the salamanders. A few of them stopped running to peer up at the confusing lines of car lights.

"A lucky thing you fellows saw 'em," the first man said. "I might've just speeded by and killed a whole batch."

"Oh, no!" protested the lady who had touched one. "Such helpless little things."

A woman in one car called out: "Helpless or not, I'm scared of them."

"No need, dearie. Here, Mister, carry a couple back to show her."

"Don't you dare!"

The first man shouted: "There's another car coming north—Lend me your flashlight and I'll wag him down."

"If we get much more of a crowd," another joked. "Someone's sure to pass the hat and take up a collection. We could call it a coffee fund for salamanders."

"Hey, that guy's coming pretty fast."

The approaching motorist suddenly noticed all the bunched cars and skidded to an abrupt halt just beyond the parked area. An anxious voice hailed us, asking if there had been a bad accident.

"No, we've got a big crowd of salamanders."

"What?" A door opened and a trucker strode into the head-lights.

"There's only a score now, but we've seen lots go by."

"Where'd they come from?"

Sid explained: "There's a big slough just west of here. The road was swarming with a hundred when Nobby,here,and I first came along."

"They look like lizards to me. Shouldn't we just kill 'em off?"

"No, no, no!" there was a general protest.

"They do a lot of good," Sid's voice rose in exasperation. "Salamanders're wonderful in gardens. They eat piles of pesky insects every summer."

"Okay, fella. Cool down. I just asked."

Three of us were now using willow branches to help the travellers on their way. A quarter hour passed, a sociable time for this assembly of strangers concerned about the welfare of the diminutive creatures. Then, with a let-down of disappointment, there were no more migrants in sight. We waited a while longer, but all the amphibians had passed this point and were now scattering unseen across the darkened landscape beyond the highway. One couple returned to their coupe and edged carefully around the remaining group and sped away. The rest of us exchanged good-nights, the first man shaking hands with us and expressing thanks for a pleasant time. Sid waited and pulled his car back onto the road at the tail end of the cavalcade of southbound cars. We could see a street light glow on the clouds ahead. Red Deer was only three miles away, where our two homes were waiting for us.

• • •

When brother Charlie and his wife, Geneva, approached their 60th anniversary a year ago, there was a flurry of excitement among our members of the family clan one weekend.

Daughter Rondo exclaimed: "It's marvelous that they've had

all those years together, but a diamond anniversary—'' She had just returned from her holidays and was financially strapped. "Diamonds are out. What about a party?"

"Not likely," I knew my brother loathed parties as much as I did. "It's my guess his Resident Daughter, as Charlie calls Marilyn, will invite them over for a special supper with her family and that'll be it."

"Aren't we going?"

Marjorie shook her head, listing various reasons including the main objection that any extra fuss would tax our octogenarian relatives' none-too-robust health at this stage.

"Surely we're going to do something?" Rondo sounded vexed. "At least we can lump our cash together and send them a decent present."

Her mother explained that as people got older they did not particularly value presents having a monetary value. Ideas were what counted, and Marjorie had already provided a suggestion.

"I hope it ties in with the celebration," Rondo turned to me. "Has it got anything to do with the years?"

"Yes, the 'diamond' part. I'm hoping to make them a diamond willow candy dish."

"Good," said our No. 1 Dot. "I'll supply the candies. They'd best be the wrapped kind, because Uncle Charlie now restricts himself to three a day."

Out in suitable woodlands a day later, I reluctantly took my eyes off a flycatcher poised on a perch between darting flights after insect food, smiled up at a boreal chickadee peering curiously down at me, cocked an ear at the stuttering pronouncements of a Tennesee warbler, then turned to the reason for this foray into a tangled willow copse a mile from home. Marjorie carried the Swede saw, while I was armed with a carpenter's hatchet and a short pruning saw. We went step after precarious step deeper into the boggy thicket, examining all diamond indentations in the gray-barked wood and rejected one prospective candy bowl-in-the-raw after another.

"This stalk would make a fine lamp," my wife indicated a gnarly piece. "Shouldn't we collect lamp blanks along the way?"

"Oh, yes." Time out was taken to clear off a few twigs to make room for saw strokes above and below the wanted material. "Lots of diamonds in this bush, though none big enough for our main purpose. Perhaps we'd better give up that hunt today and just collect lamp and candle-stick stalks until our haversacks are full. Another day we'll explore a different woodland and hope for larger willow trunks."

We had the pleasure of two more hunts. There were extra bonuses of finding a cluster of edible mushrooms, startling a doe deer from a day-bed, and peeping into the spider-web bound nest of a red-eyed vireo. Finally we found an appropriate willow pattern with a gracefully swooped diamond hollow and well flared outer lips. Naturally, it was located in a wretchedly cramped place. Nearly an hour passed before the confined strokes of the pruning saw severed the wanted piece. It was cut longer above and below the desired bowl part to avoid any splitting, also to give me solid hand-holds on the shaft during the diamond clearing part of the potential candy bowl.

"How long will it take you to make the dish?" Marjorie asked. "The anniversary date is about two months away."

"A month at least," I thought of the four sizes of half-moon gouges, the different knives for skiving, the multiple grades of sandpaper needed before applying a finish coat. On the next free spare time I got the bowl started and at once had a problem. "The clearing gouge slipped—I'll have to go deep down to smooth out that mistake. And the high curved lip we hoped would be bright yellow has turned out creamy instead."

Rondo came visiting from her Edmonton home, full of telephone news about No. 2. Dot Heather and son Greg in distant U.S. towns. We listened, had lunch, listened again and went out to the garden. A new patch of purslane weeds had popped up, which meant trowel work and a crick in the back before all tops and roots of the fleshy plants could be dumped into the incinerator. Marjorie and Rondo took turns at shuffle-hoeing the flowers while I hilled the spuds. There were family walks to viewpoints, exchanges of fresh jokes, dawdling time over supper and book talk. Indeed, the whole weekend passed without any of us glancing once at the candy dish.

Six weeks later gouging and sandpapering work had been finished, though the stalk was still in the long piece for easy handling. The time had come to shed the waste ends. The largest vise was opened wide, the bowl wrapped in protective leather to prevent denting, then jaws tightened and the first diagonal cut was successfuly made and the unwanted part dropped clear. The bowl was reversed in the vise and the fine-toothed saw worked again. Halfway down, the blade slithered much too easily through the heart of the wood. When the waste piece dropped off, I was dismayed to see a gaping hole of half rotted wood at the newly exposed end. Marjorie sympathized.

"Too bad. You haven't time to find and make another, either. The rest is quite attractive, Nobby. Can't you plug it?"

I felt sure patching would spoil the bowl's appearance. The diamond anniversary now loomed ominously near on the calendar horizon. Rondo had telephoned the night before that when the official 60th date came due, she would arrive on that weekend to carry the finished article the final part of the journey for personal delivery to my brother and sister-in-law in Calgary.

"Well, I'll sand the ends and apply the polish," I said regretfully. "We'll tell Rondo to ask Charlie and Geneva to place this holey part next a wall where it won't be seen."

Marjorie gave me a cheerful nod and returned to the house. When I went in later, she was making a mouse. It had an elongated pebble for a body, flaps of gray felt for protruding ears, large pupil-rotating eyes, a stub of an impudent nose with a wisp of a leather tail cocked up triumphantly at the rear.

"This will take care of the hole," she beamed at the finished creation. "He'll be guardian of the bowl's cave."

All was made ready, the congratulatory card signed, and Rondo fully approved of everything when she arrived before the fancy wrapping stage. A note of explanation was written about not wishing to waste nearly two full months of hobby time, adding that if they did not care for the bowl and mouse, they could at least eat the candy therein and confine the willow dish to their daughter Marilyn's fireplace.

"They're really pleased," Rondo said on the return trip. "Mom, everybody loved the artificial mouse, and Unk Charlie said the bowl's much too nice to burn. Marilyn wanted to claim it right away for display on her mantlepiece, but Charlie told her in his most ghoulish tones to wait for the due process of last wills and testaments. Meanwhile, Uncle has hidden the candy to prevent Geneva getting more than her fair share. Dad, he sent you a secret message, which I now hand over."

It was a four-lined verse of unknown authorship, as follows:

> *Diamond weddings are not common,*
> *The percentage is quite small;*
> *Married life can't last forever—*
> *It's a good world, after all!*

The Big-Booted Firemen

During our ten-month sojourn in Lethbridge the family discovered that my father was something of a pyromaniac. There happened to be a grass-covered plot between our house and the home occupied by a large Ukrainian lady who regarded us with scowling suspicion because of my mother's strange way of mangling English. We could have said as much about our neighbour's treatment of the language, which amounted to "Allo" in the morning and "Far-well" at night. The sum total of all she addressed directly to me, minus the adjectives, consisted of two words: "Go 'way."

The neglected quackgrass had grown rank during the summer and offended my father's eyes. I was curious about the Ukrainian lady's poultry, since the birds' runway extended right across the back end of the vacant lot and abutted our vegetable garden. From the safety of our turnip patch I had close-ups of her ever-hungry hens. As she flung oats to the clustered fowl from the doorway of the ramshackle coop, she glared ferociously across at me and shook a fat fist as she shouted "Go 'way." Even so, the Allos and Far-wells and Go 'ways remained fairly neutral until that windy Saturday when my father could no longer abide the sight of all that dead grass. He dropped a lighted match on the upwind end of the property, nodded his approval as it flared, then proceeded down the basement to fetch a pail of water for fireguard duty.

A boy named Carter and I witnessed this. We were delighted with the instant blaze and sudden roar of wind-driven fire, but our appreciative study of the scene was rudely interrupted by an uncouth roar from the neighbour lady. She pelted from her kitchen in a fury of passion and wielded a broom on the far edge of the advancing fire, all the while shouting words in her own language that sounded very much off-colour. At this juncture my mother charged out of our house armed with a wet floor mop.

"Dinna stand idle," she scolded us. "Help put it oot!"

Carter grabbed a handful of dirt and threw it in the general direction of the fire, I followed his example and our enjoyment of the spectacle continued unabated. In all, there could have been less than five minutes of action, because it was not a wide lot and the bottom end was cut off by the presence of the sprawling chicken run. Those chickens uttered terrified ka-fuffles, their unlordly rooster cowering in the hen house entry with one frightened eye staring out at the swiftly approaching doom.

"They're goners," Carter declared.

"Who's goners?"

"The chickens—When feathers catch fire, they're goners."

He seemed elated at the prospect. My mother was wheezing in the smoky center of the fire but never slackened her vigorous mop blows left and right. She had breath enough left to hurl Scottish insults back at whatever profanity the large neighbour yelped. If it was not Ukrainian profanity, then our childish perceptions were seriously out of whack. Carter and I belatedly realized we were not effective on the upwind part and raced around to flank my mother's position and stamped our small shoes at the hot flames. Our combined efforts were rewarded. Backed against the runway wires, we battlers stopped the blaze in time to save the cackling chickens, endangered coop, and cowardly rooster. And then, to the utter astonishment of us boys, the two women fell upon each other's necks and hugged and sobbed in unison, all the while praising each other for their putting out tactics.

"Come awa' in," my mother concluded. "Tak' tea wi' us."

"Yah, tanks, goot!" replied the other, beaming.

"Us too?" asked the alert Carter.

At that ultimate moment, with the parched yellow grass burned down to black ground, my father came up from the basement with half a pail of water and an old gunny sack. He paused on the doorstep, surveyed the lot that had affronted his neat habits, and nodded his pleasure at this new turn of events. Then he went back into the house to dispose of his extinguishing equipment.

• • •

So far as can be remembered, he never indulged his craze for lighting grass during the years we lived in Calgary. It was a different matter after we reached Red Deer. The potato acreage had to be burned clean before plough and harrows arrived. However, no harm was done by those early spring blazes, because snow still lingered at field edges and damp grass was easily controlled. There was an accomplishment about those fires, a nice comradeship as we stood together at the edges next our ready sprinkling cans. My mother kept well away from us, not wishing to aggravate her asthma. At last we had all the potential crop areas scorched bald, then the farmer with the Clyde team and implements came and prepared the land for planting. After the harassing event of harvest, piles of withered tan-hued potato haulms placed in the middle of each empty field smoldered slowly without danger to the surroundings.

The boy years passed, and for a while our home was located north of the South School. There were three vacant lots between our house and the school, all sporting rank growth. One day my father applied a match to the grassy expanse just as pupils were released for their mid-morning recess. The dry fodder caught, a breeze quickened and drove the red-yellow dancers straight at the school where children stopped their play to watch in excited fascination. My mother's frantic warning called me from my typewriter. I saw the two teachers hurry out of the South School with buckets of tap water which they tossed from the vantage point of the porch, barely missing their juvenile charges with the spray. Three neighbours quickly joined me in a desperate effort to control the blaze and douse it.

My father, noting that the conflagration needed no further encouragement from him, went indoors and calmly brewed himself a cup of tea.

"Och, Willie!" my mother reproached him after the emergency was over and she had invited the fire-fighters in for scones. "Willie, ye might ha'e burnt doon the school an' half the toon."

"I think the children were on Mr. Wood's side," one neighbour said. "I noticed they were cheering during the worst of the fire, but they became gloomy after it was out. Only the teachers thanked us."

My father poured tea for all on that occasion, while my bustling mother filled everybody with jam-covered scones and wedges of iced layer cake. When we were alone as a family unit again, there was both irritation and despair in her recriminations, throughout which my father insisted the vacant lots looked much better as a result of the purifying burn.

"A-weel, frae noo on every time ye reach fer a match, I'll be feart o' the consequences."

Time and again she had sufficient reason to be frightened, because my father kept lighting dead grass whenever the adventurous bug bit him.

• • •

His most impressive achievement in this matter came a few years after my mother's death. Marjorie and I had bought another Red Deer home surrounded by a large lot measuring two acres in extent and Papa Willie lived with us. Our brick house commanded a pleasant view of a creek, a cement bridge, and distant traffic on the main thoroughfare. Behind the house was an adequately large garden space in my father's care, beyond this cultivated patch a sizeable grassy area which he kept eyeing in speculation. One day he carried a small basin from the house, filled it at the outside hose tap, and carried it towards the garden. I assumed he was going to water one of his special bulbs and accepted the offer of a car ride to the town post office. We were almost there when the eerie wail of the fire siren moaned out from the city hall roof. A sudden revelation flashed into my head about the reason for the basin of water in my father's hands.

"Please drive back at once!"

We easily beat the fire truck getting there. Both of us grabbed wet sacks from worried Marjorie and went to work. The lady residing to the north, due to produce her second child any moment, waddled out of harm's way upwind to seek a safe haven. Another neighbour joined us in the frantic job, while my father refilled the wash basin time and again and exclaimed something that sounded like an explosive "Pshaw!" as firemen raced across his neat garden on their way to the fire engine.

The driver had come hooting and screaming from the station and aimed the handsome brassy machine at the smoke. Unfortunately, from the main avenue the smoke appeared to be well behind our house. The driver completely circled the block and approached us from the far side where the heavily laden truck bogged down in a spinster lady's garden. It remained there, too, wedged to its hubcaps in the soft earth with members of the brigade heaving and shoving lustily at their in-operative apparatus. Our emergency force of three got the fire under control without the help of a single fireman. At last, by sheer strength of numbers and roaring motor, the brigade shifted the truck out of the sweet pea patch and sped townward away from the outraged sput-terings of the indignant spinster.

These disasterous happenings left me with a hollow apprehen-sion in my midriff.

"We'll likely receive a steep bill for calling out the brigade," I confided my fears to Marjorie.

"We didn't call them," she replied. "I'm glad someone did, and I suspect it was the expectant mother. In any case, none of the firemen helped put out the fire. You and your friends did that."

My father came into the house and brusquely interrupted our conversation, his goatee bristling with anger. He demanded that I accompany him outside, where he pointed at the large footprints indented all over his beloved garden.

"It's disgraceful," he said. "They didn't even try to avoid it. By going a few yards north, they could have spared me all this havoc."

At the moment I did not offer him any sympathy. Instead, still mopping my sweaty brow, I excused myself from looking at any more of the impressive boot-prints and went upstairs for a much needed bath. Having changed into fresh clothing, I proceeded resolutely to the city office and had audience with the commissioner.

"I understand your position," he smiled. "The fire chief has just finished telling me about their error. His driver had no idea there was so much vacant space behind your home. By the way, would you be interested in subdividing the burnt over part to provide us with more building lots?"

• • •

As I write, young hummingbirds have now left home nests and our scarlet-petalled feeder is constantly visited by the ethereal birds. The buzzing fights of adults during early summer have ended, ruby-throated males departing our area a few days ago. Quarrels among the sprites remaining often break out, especially whenever two hummers try to share one perch to get at the syrup. Often there have been four feeding at the available florets, with three others hovering nearby. Where else but in our tree-screened sanctuary could Marjorie step outdoors in her pyjamas at nine o'clock of a summer evening to bring in and refill the feeder? While she was indoors the tiny birds chittered protesting squeaks at the empty hook, whirling inches from Marjorie's head when she carried the feeder back to the holder.

On the morning of August 8th, 1985, rain drubbed steadily down in gray sheets. When we first opened the bedroom window at dawn and looked out at the lacy fronds of elder, one hummingbird was perched close to the glass under the protection of the eaves, while other twigs sheltered a chickadee and a clay-coloured sparrow within scant inches of our eyes. Feeling the gush of warmer air from the quietly opened window, the chickadee came directly to the fly screen and flattened itself on the wire mesh, obviously getting comfort from the released house heat. We went through to the front room and drew the drapes to examine the hummer feeder suspended outside, where all four perches were occupied by hungry mites. They were busy sucking up nectar through their hollow tongues, so near us that we could see the swift pumping of their hearts. Five others hovered above and below the feeder.

Nine hummers in sight at one time, plus the tenth perched near the bedroom window. As we watched there were dramatic flarings of spread tails, menacing dashes at perchers, frequently two birds would rise beak to beak with whirling wings and go up and away out of sight. But hunger on this chilly morning soon brought them back to the feeder, where satiated first-comers eventually flew off to the birch tree to shake and preen, scratch and huffle their iridescent feathers and await a further chance to guzzle.

"Fun to see," murmured Marjorie when we withdrew to start our day.

"If this wet spell lasts, they'll leave for the south within the week."

"We can only wish them safe journeys."

Next morning all but three of the hummers had left our region. We thought of their long trip ahead of them, following the flower trails across Canada and the States, their non-stop flight across the Gulf of Mexico for five hundred exhausting miles. On farther still, some to pause on tropical islands of the Caribbean and others to go as far as the orchid forests of the Amazon River basin in Brazil.

Not a Drop

When we first moved to this property, within 24 hours the well ran dry. After the new one was drilled, a sudden explosion revealed the presence of sweet gas somewhere down the 310-foot hole. A small edition of those bobbing-head oil rig pumps operates our well, with a removable wooden plank platform above the motor and shaft. In winter we place a neat arrangement of insulation batts on the planks to keep everything below protected from the frosty air another six feet above. At ground or surface level there is the covering of a thick cement slab, and once there was a twenty-inch square piece of cast iron as cap to permit a working entrance to and from the mechanical apparatus.

After a normal day's use of the well for baths, rinses, filling the kettle, cooking and pot cleaning, dish-washing, and all the assorted water requirements of the household, sweet gas would seep up the long well shaft from its hidden lair and start accumulating in the motor part of the dual cavities. Gradually this gas would get more dense as day became night. A final visit to the little room at bedtime, a last flush activated the pump, then —

PPPPOOOOOOOOWWWWWWWWWWWWWWW-WWWWWWWWW!!!!!

The motor spark had ignited the collected gas and it exploded with a terrifically loud boom and a wrenching sound of smashed fence boards. The 40-pound hunk of cast iron which sealed the concrete top away from inquisitive mice went cavorting wildly through the air and knocked off boards en route to a resting place away out yonder on the meadow. Always it blew eastward, a fortunate direction for us because there the heavy iron had lots of roaming room. If it had sailed westward, the metal square would have crashed into the house itself and shattered windows and walls, perhaps even inflicting havoc upon our cringing persons.

Whenever there was an explosion, whoever was in residence would grab gowns, flip on the back porch light, then dash out to stare in dismay at wisps of smoke curling up from that square hole where the iron cap should have been. With the aid of flashlights, the family would peer down into the well to see what was askew. After the iron cover had been retrieved and put in place, we returned indoors and tested the taps. Each gasped convulsively for air but yielded nothing more. Which brought about our eleven o'clock-at-night realization that we didn't have a drop of water in the house, save for two scanty cupfuls in the tea kettle.

Next morning as soon as farm neighbours stirred to do chores, we would borrow a five-gallon cream can full of the required fluid and try to manage. Meanwhile, the receptionist at the busy plumber's office eight miles away cheerfully told us, "Yes, Of Course!" We were next on their list of favoured customers who were going to get their services.

"Perhaps even tomorrow afternoon, if the boys can manage it."

Our very first emergency awakened in me a mental picture of a bygone convenience. There followed a frantic search for boards and plyboard, with a sheet of tin exactly the right size for the back of a hastily constructed out-house set above an axed and shovelled hole. It was fitted with a plastic seat discarded from a modern bowl. Because of the tin back, this privy sometimes produced devastating echoes and was dubbed "The Thunderer." Yet it served until we could engage a real carpenter to build us a more suitable reserve building.

Meanwhile the well had been mended, though the problem was by no means cured and another trio of blasts rocked our sanities. From these bombastic happenings there developed the idea of building a wooden cap with a fly-screened ventilator poked up, topped with a wide-eaved roof to replace the now retired heavy iron capping. The fly-screen was not only to keep out flies, but to prevent wasps from building in our vital underground structure and viciously sealing off our well from any servicing by those elite among tradesmen, the plumbers.

A plumber's mate disdainfully examined my wooden ventilator and suggested that any tinsmith could fashion a more ornate and durable model for us. This was done, and I converted the former upright part of the wooden structure into a four-roomed purple martin colony box. European starlings found the compartments alluring and in three days' time filled them with nesting materials. We greatly dislike starlings and their pugnacious harassment of beneficial birds that use boxes, so starlings were allowed to finish just the first phase of their nesting.

I then made "converters." These were small rectangles of plywood complete with inch-and-a-quarter entry holes. They were tacked overtop of the two-inch holes I had drilled so hopefully into our erstwhile well ventilator in hopes of attracting martins. The starlings came back with final beakfuls of feathers to line their nests, stuck their heads through the much smaller converter openings, kicked, shoved, pushed and squawked ever so many bird blasphemies. No matter how hard they struggled, they could not enter through the converter openings. After a five minute hassle, they rested on doorsteps and peered around and individually said to themselves something like this:

"I got the grass and rootlets in there, because I can see them. I've lined the cup with fine twigs and poplar fuzz and even cow hairs from farms, but now—I can't get in!"

They cackled at each other in ways that informed the surroundings that there were many unladylike thoughts inside their assorted heads. Eventually they stopped fuming and once more vigorously tried to get past the shoulder-blocking converter holes, with no success. Again the birds gathered on the porch ledges, glancing around the landscape with never a suspicion that I was chuckling behind the kitchen curtains with binoculars trained on them. I could almost see the wheels spinning around behind their intent eyes.

"I just know this is the nest I built," went the starling's thoughts. "I particularly remember that large branch-twig at the back; I must've carried it half a mile and it nearly bent my beak. There were three long days of searching for all that fine bundle of materials. I remember being pleased with the accomplishment and looked forward to setting there for umpteen days to hatch out my eggs . . . EGGS!! Oh, where can I lay my urgent eggs?"

There followed a tense moment, the birds exchanged meaningful looks with one another and a terrible thought circulated among them.

"This place is jinxed!"

With one accord they flew away and never came back to the haunted bird box that season. In the autumn I would remove the converters, clean out the nests, and let another batch of starlings try the same oust-the-martin tactics next year.

• • •

Purple martins have been mistakenly shot for starlings in several parts of Canada and the United States, and our martin boxes began to stand forlorn and neglected as the years went by, except for the pesky starlings shooed off spring after spring until . . .

"We'd best take down our three twelve-roomers and the old ventilator and just concentrate on bird boxes that really work, the ones for tree swallows, bluebirds, chickadees, and nesting shelves for robins."

The multi-roomed boxes were removed, with memories crowding back to 1919 when my boy-made boxes poked up and on April 28th of every spring a flock of purple martins swooped in. They chortled excitedly and went in and out of every room in happy anticipation of finding a different place to colonize. It started a love affair with martins that endured since my 11th year. Now no martins come to our sanctuary though we visit the city hall park every summer where a few martins still nest.

Our well problems did not end with the installation of a sheet metal ventilator. The gas still accumulated and occasionally exploded, not drastically and loudly as of yore because of the ventilator, yet bad enough in that it often interrupted the functions of the pump. Out would saunter a whistling plumber to put us back on stream. Finally a blessed member of their group solved our sweet gas outbursts.

"What you need here is a spark-free motor, then the gas would have no way of getting lit. It would just have to seep off harmlessly through the ventilator."

The expensive remedy was well worth our freedom from booms. Even so, now and then a cable wire would fracture, an important belt break, and off we'd hurry once again to neighbours and fill every container on hand with water. We began keeping two large plastic containers full of stored water for emergency flushings, though we rarely use them. Of a summer's day it is much easier to walk outside to the discreetly placed old fashioned back house with its pleasant open door view of birds' nests and rabbits snoozing in their forms. First, of course, with the mutual consent of house people of no trespassing out that way for a few minutes.

Winter is different. It became sadly true that every time the well went on the blink during frigid weather, those people in residence developed constipation. This state became almost chronic until the plumber's truck had come and gone. We have discussed this aspect of rural living with our town friends. Most of them think the whole complicated affair is somewhat amusing. A few have managed to spare us a modicum of sympathy, especially our winter season health problem.

Lorren Taylor offered this advice: "The best cure for constipation is to sit on a large round of cheese and swallow a live mouse."

• • •

Which reminds me. Near the end of May, 1985, we drove to town and picked up his wife, Kay, who has become familiar with most of the new "Walks" scattered along the miles of the beautifully conceived Waskasoo Park. It was six o'clock of a cool, foggy morning, hence we decided to drive to Heritage Ranch and there left the car, starting our walk on the higher paths of what used to be called the Hoopfer Property. In my memory it was Mr. Opie's farm; somewhere in the early 1920's a large part of his holdings were unbroken and enclosed by a loop of the Red Deer River. This scrubland flat became famous as the site of Alberta's first Gilwell Scout Leaders Training Camp. A trainer from South Africa instructed over a score of men in crafts and lore of Scouting as it was practiced at that time.

I did not attend the camp, being busy writing for boys' magazines. Mr. James Gall, organizer and leader of the Second Troop of local Scouts, enrolled and was amused that the instructor asked them to help cure his habit of chewing on juicy ends of timothy.

"Whenever you see me pluck one, yell out."

Mr. Gall decided this was really an observation test for those taking the Gilwell course, basing his judgement on the fact that it was part of a second class scout's Kim's Game. The "Kim" name was from Kipling's book about that young character who took detailed note of everything and everybody. Scoutmasters in our period devised a form of Kim's Game by jotting down contents of a store window on the way to the weekly meeting. Jewelry stores with about 30 items on display were considered good. At the meeting's end, on the way home boys were accompanied to the selected window and given one minute to stare in and try to memorize everything in view. Then they were walked to another street light to write out items recalled; if a boy could corrently name twenty of the thirty things displayed, he passed. An overly astute boy made a private daytime survey of store windows and wrote out lists for each. At test time he cribbed from his notes and got a perfect score every time. Yet when this same boy was tested with an assortment of items during a weekend camping trip, he failed miserably. His duplicity was confessed and the boy was chagrined to learn he had violated a scout's most sacred code of honour.

On those bygone camping expeditions up or down the river shores, we left town on Friday an hour after school and returned home by supper time on Sunday. Each boy carried a 15-pound pack, a safe load limit for boys averaging 12 to 14 years old. Each load was made up of six pounds of dry food ingredients such as flour, rice, macaroni, prunes, bacon, dried apples and seasonings. Another six pounds was allowed for sleeping gear; at that time there were no lightweight sleeping bags in stores, so one boy of every pair carried one blanket and a groundsheet, while his chum lugged along two blankets and together they shared the groundsheet and bedding. Then there were the shelters, two pounds for half a pup tent. They were the button-together type, open ended and very second-hand, bought from an Ontario war surplus store that stocked Boer War left-overs. Only one pound was conceded for toothbrush, comb, knife, pad and pencil and one spare pair of socks.

The leader carried a heavier pack because he had the burden of a large first aid kit to serve all 30 boys attending. In my own case I carried extra fishing lines and hooks to outfit any youngsters keen on angling. In addition, there were chocolate bars and candy suckers to be distributed as prizes for the speediest tent slingers, best cooks, any boy who could gather the most berries or catch the most fish. The boys trusted me in our First Troop to identify wild food to supplement what we carried. Plants such as pigweed, dandelion leaves and plantain, mushrooms, wild currant leaves for tea making, and the berries in season.

We carried thumbsticks instead of the traditional clumsy scout staves, using the Y-topped thumbsticks of sturdy black birch to serve double duty as helpers on hill climbs, also to act as tent posts when in camp. Tent pegs were fashioned from driftwood branches handy to sites. If mosquitoes were pesty and we had to choose a wide sandbar to avoid them, rocks were used to anchor the pup tent sides and guy roof ropes leading from front and back thumbstick posts.

There were tests. Tenderfoot boys were required to learn a few Scout laws, flag signalling, some useful knots, and elementary health care. Second class scouts progressed through many more skills up the scale toward a first class badge, eventually getting a King's Scout golden emblem if the required number of proficiency badges had been earned. There had to be alterations in the original English rules, modified to suit Alberta conditions. There was the further complication that I was barely a year older than my charges and yet was held fully responsible for their welfare and lives. It seemed important to stress that the chief purpose of our outings was to revel in good fellowship and laughter as we soaked up as much camp craft as time permitted.

* * *

So 60 and more years after that Gilwell Scout Leaders Course on Mr. Opie's farm flat, Kay Taylor, Wife Marjorie and I set out from the new Heritage Ranch parking lot to walk over the territory again, now criss-crossed with trails, picnic spots, garbage bins and ponds. We were eager to visit places we fondly remembered from younger years. My troop had camped there many times, Kay had probably walked there with Lorren years ago, and Marjorie and I had visited the lovely region several times during our courting days (or daze).

When the Depression hit in 1929 even before we started courting, I was earning sufficient monetary returns from many juvenile magazines, but because of a recent experience of living off the land for twenty months I was acutely sympathetic toward the thin, raggedly dressed gangs of men who were called Hoboes. They dropped off the freight trains a quarter-mile south of the Red Deer CPR station to camp in the Hobo Jungle alongside Waskasoo Creek. There they shared whatever food had been begged from kindly house-wives along Victoria Avenue, some coming as far east as the South School suburb where our family home was located. It was easy for me to get an invitation to visit the Jungle with an offer to show them the nearest berry patches and best fishing holes. One never went to the Hobo Jungle without taking along vegetables from our own and neighbours' gardens, cans of pork and beans and, if funds were flush, an assortment of canned fruit, and always lots of bread and butter.

One man among the many hundreds who stopped at the Jungle became a closer acquaintance. He walked with me out to Opie's farm and said he was weary of being bunched in with a hundred men in freight cars or in distant and local versions of the Hobo Jungle. Being a bit of a loner myself, I understood his feelings. Mr. Opie readily agreed to let the man camp at the south end of the flats and together we rigged up a lean-to shelter where he could spend the night. He followed me along the boulder strewn path hugging the river shore under the towering banks bordering the Cronquist farm, where we caught enough goldeyes for his supper and breakfast.

He enjoyed his stay so much that he remained there, building an open-faced Adirondack-style hut about eight feet long, six high and seven deep. The walls and roof were framed with dead branches over which he shingled moss from the thickly carpeted forest floor, another layer of branches overtop served to anchor the moss. His original bedroll consisted of a tattered piece of canvas and a coarse blanket, but the Salvation Army produced a flannelette sheet, a woollen blanket and a cot pallet as mattress. There were many helpful people around then, as now.

My friend was comfortable there during the summer. He made wire novelties for house-to-house sales to earn money for his extras. Galvanized wire was bent into various household gadgets, the most popular of these being a window holder-upper, a simple double twist of wire that commanded a 3 for 10-cent price. A broom holder was more complicated and cost 15 cents; even more difficult to make, but easier to sell, was a handled sealer-lifter, at a time when the steam processing of preserves was an annual autumn chore for housewives. Our man mildly prospered with his wire wares and passed several contented weeks there on Opie's Flat, until a letter came to urge him back to his Ontario home because of a death in the family. Before he left Red Deer, he made the rounds to thank those who had helped him in our district, and there had been many.

• • •

Kay had been along the Heritage Ranch trails before and guided us down the log-supported steps to the floor of the old Gilwell Flat, now densely solid with mature spruces, tall balms and aspens, clumps of willow and buck brush. The undergrowth was thick with jointed rush, cinquefoil, wolf berry and kinnikinic. The sun flashed out from behind a shroudy cloud, setting the birds to singing. During our walk we saw and heard over thirty species, ranging from spotted sandpipers to belted kingfishers, many warblers and vireos intermingled with the strident 'chonk-a-lee-ree' call of a red-winged blackbird. All the while we were deep in murmured conversation about whatever was topical, and three hours winged swiftly past before we climbed to the highlands again to our parked car.

Back at the Taylor home we breakfasted heartily, in the midst of which Lorren himself came back from his morning coffee break with the Geriatric Club. He told us of their latest arguments and decisions, including the possible distribution of car stickers that read:

"Out of Date, but Out of Debt!"

Ice Cream Cones

One snowy night last winter Marjorie and I elected to watch the TV news. In addition to current terrors of world affairs, the station gave coverage to another city's indoor rodeo. Not only bronc busting, steer wrestling, and rope-jerking insults meted out to frightened calves, but many close-up views of a tame Brahma bull. There was camera footage of the docile animal being paraded into busy shopping malls and through store aisles. Due precautions of strips of carpet material had been laid out before and gathered up after each part of the processions, so that the placid beastie would not slip on tile floors or otherwise offend anyone's sensibilities.

Pictures of this amiable member of the Taurus family triggered memories of my first close-up look at a bull. It happened at Red Deer's fair, a summer when the exhibition board members decided to award boywork to local boyscouts, recently organized. The scoutmaster had appointed me to be one of five patrol leaders, each in charge of seven boys. Uniformly hatted, shirted and neckerchiefed, very conscious of our new shorts and bare pink knees, all 35 boys of First Troop gathered outside the exhibition grounds office of the fair board. While we nervously waited for officialdom to remember their promise to us, two elderly ladies spotted me and drew me to one side.

"Nobby, if you're after a job, please come and work for us.

Our group is in charge of the grandstand booth this summer. Pick out three of your friends and come.''

The scoutmaster consented and four of us followed the women through a side entrance to the grandstand enclosure. A weather-beaten booth stood at one side, squared in with boards halfway up each side, the over-hanging roof providing shade and smelling of recently applied tar paper. A large white banner was draped across the countered front with black lettered W.C.T.U. blazoned thereon.

"We've got a double concession, both for the grandstand and all standing room within the fenced area. We'd like you boys to be our salesmen, going up into the bleachers and around the standing people to sell soft drinks and ice cream cones, and sandwiches. For every 5-cent cone you sell, we'll allow you a half-cent commission, the same for 5-cent bottles of lemonade, but for the 15-cent sandwiches, you'll earn 2 cents each. Perhaps it doesn't sound like much, but if you work hard you'll make lots of spending money.''

They studied us expectantly. My boys held a whispering conference with me. Apart from the commissions, the prospect of seeing grandstand shows free of charge was most tempting. We nodded our heads in eager agreement with the ladies' offer; we were willing to be their perambulating salesmen.

"Then be here at one o'clock sharp. Grandstand gates open then, though performances don't start for another hour. We'd like you to be ready for early arrivals. Now go to your homes and eat lunches, but be sure to be back here on time.''

It was a roasting end of July day, the Fahrenheit temperature hovering around 95 degrees. One boy said that on such a hot day people would want lots of pop drinks and we'd become millionaires. The ladies smiled benignly at this outburst and we scattered our several ways.

My mother nodded approval of the proposed job.

"When ye finish tendin' the chookies and coo, come in and wash and eat a big dinner. Wurrrk verra hard at the fair, and mayhap ye'll earn a wee bit o' siller.''

As I fed the chickens and took Bessie to a different pasture, my mind puzzled over the bold lettering and I asked my parents about the sign.

"Does W.C.T.U. stand for a secret society?"

"Na, they're just the temperance ladies. Bow yer head fer Grace."

The blistering sun beat down unmercifully that afternoon. There were greasy odours from the midway restaurant tent pitched beyond the grandstand area's high board fence. That barrier did not block out brassy tunes blaring from the merry-go-round and whip-rides, nor shouts of barkers in front of the lion's den, freak pavilion, snake pit, and monkey house. For the first fidgety minutes we boys eyed the ever-increasing numbers of people coming through the grandstand stiles, trying to calculate if the hot looking crowd would buy produce from us. My wily companions, noting that bleacher seats were in the shade, requested that they serve patrons there. This left me in sole possession of the standing-room-only crowd.

"You may start now," the lady in charge said. One younger, more muscular woman worked with a scoop to fill the cones, these being placed in a metal container holding twelve. Two boys took the six-pack pop bottles, while one volunteered to serve ham sandwiches, leaving me the cones. "I've written your names on separate sheets, boys, and I'll keep track of all sales. Shout your wares; don't be shy."

Our voices were feeble amid all the other audible competition, yet at sight of my ice cream people reached into pockets. Sales were brisk among the standers, even after a clown climbed the steps onto the raised wooden platform in front. He introduced the afternoon performance of acrobats, jugglers, a couple of sketchily clad dancing girls who also tried to sing, followed by trained dogs jumping through hoops. I caught only an occasional glimpse of the various acts. Farmers had clustered along the race track fence near the grandstand enclosure and waved me over, there I emptied holder after holder during the afternoon.

"It's for a worthy cause," one lady said to another when they discovered I was going beyond the enclosure. "Carry on, Nobby."

Before supper I had a refreshing bath in a galvanized tub of well water at home, returning to the grandstand at seven o'clock as required. Heat lightning was off in the distance, forecasting thunder on that humid evening. People standing around the enclosure were happy to buy cones as diversions to alleviate their foot-weary discomforts, so the evening sales were almost as brisk as during the sweltering afternoon. When O Canada was sung at half past ten and The King to end the performance, the booth ladies were wilted with fatigue but managed wan smiles as we handed in empty containers, money aprons, and spoke our good-nights.

The threatened storm did not come, and heat seemed more oppressive on the second and final afternoon. Sales soared. I concentrated on selling cones rather than carrying heavy pop bottles around my territory. The race track became busy between grandstand acts with half-mile, pony, and Indian races. Farmers, racehorse owners, assorted workers and hangers-on were lined three and four deep along the fence near the grandstand. A judges' tower reared up on the inside part of the oval opposite the stage platform. One of those judges ordered me off the track, but farmers shouted him down and continued to hold out nickels for cones.

"What's happening at the far part of the track?" a booth lady asked as I mopped my brow under the hot scout hat.

"The stock's getting lined up for a parade," I answered, having heard the farmers talk. "They say the parade will finish off the afternoon show."

The woman who had manipulated the cone-scooper wore out, but the husband of another lady volunteered to serve. His fresh energy speeded the process and sales doubled. I ran between booth and cone prospects, trying to keep up with demands of spectators stifling under the pitiless sun. Mooings from restless cattle, bleatings of sheep, nickerings of horses sounded from the far curve of the track oval, the races being finished for that season. Side-show racket lulled as midway operators rested before the anticipated business rush when the bulging grandstand spewed out its crowd.

At last the parade rounded the near bend and came into view. It was led by a group of mounted riders prancing ahead of the swaggering Clyde and Belgian draft horse teams which pulled drays loaded with sheep and swine. Slower brood mares and foals followed, the lumbering cattle at the rear. Even as excitement soared over this display of the district agriculture's finest, watchers wanted more ice cream. I was dimly aware of bursts of applause when the fair board secretary used a megaphone to announce the names of grand championship and first class winners as the various sections went by, but my chief concern was handing out cones and making change and putting coins in the canvas apron the ladies had provided.

"Here come the cattle," I heard one stockman say.

"Give me four," called someone farther along. He got my final stock of that dozen and I hurried boothward for replacements. Soon I was on my way again, crossing the fence to serve the farmers. Three newly-packed cones had been distributed and I was reaching out a fourth to a burly man when he drew hastily back. Others suddenly jerked away from the fence. Someone shouted a warning:

"Behind you, boy—mad bull!"

I spun around to see the curved black horns of a Jersey bull pointed at me, a bellowing roar swelling from the animal's open throat as it lunged to skewer me. Before it could strike, I jammed the cone smack into its gaping mouth. The bull reared back and shuddered to a trembling stop, the merest hint of its head weight leaning on my small chest. While it gagged on the ice cream, the worried owner panted close and grabbed the dangling control stick attached to the nose-ring. The animal gulped convulsively, shook its massive head in what seemed like frustration, then quietly followed the man back into the line of parade. I wiped my slavered hand on the canvas apron and turned dazedly back toward the W.C.T.U. booth, not even aware that the cone container emptied itself during my walk. Yet it was proved later that the exact amount of change had been deposited properly by eight honest customers. Booth ladies fussed over me.

"Do you know about bulls' tongues?" I asked them. "It's rougher than sandpaper." This provoked tears from some as other more practical women sponged my hand and arm clean and gave my face a towelling. They sat me down on one of their two chairs and fed me a high-piled cone and told me there was no charge for it. At the night end of a long and somewhat disjointed day, after both Auld Lang Syne and God Save the King had been sung by the grandstand crowd, which then gave itself three rousing cheers, the booth lady in charge drew me aside.

"I don't want the other boys to see, because you've earned double. It's all in small coins, so I've put them into a bag. I'll pin it inside your shirt pocket for safe keeping. And Nobby, go home at once. Don't look at sideshows or fortune wheels—go straight home."

The best possible advice for one dreadfully tired small boy. The hill path through the dark spruces had never seemed steeper; there were many halts along the way to pant, to look up beyond the tree tops to glimmering stars above. I became renewed in vigor as home came in sight. There, to the delight of my mother, the jingling contents of the bag were spilled with dramatic abandon onto the kitchen table where nickels, dimes, and quarters scattered into a silvery, rattling heap.

"The lady said there's seven dollars here," I announced in triumph. "We're rich!"

After her counting had confirmed the figure, my mother sorted out some nickels and dimes.

"I'll let you keep fifty cents for each day."

I was elated; a whole dollar, all to myself. Never had I been so wealthy at one time and was vastly content with this reward for two days of intense cone salesmanship. Nor did I bother to dream of dagger-like bull horns when I tumbled into bed.

Next morning my father came down with a summer cold. His face was flushed, he panted for breath, and his head ached. Not once did he reach for a book to read.

"Och, Willie, sup yer porridge. Mind the auld remedy? It's starve a fever, stuff a cold."

"I hab a feber," my father muttered.

"Na, na, it's a cold," my mother dosed him with Epsom salts and forced him to swallow glasses of water containing lemon juice. Against all his protests, she wrapped blankets around him and moved his chair next the kitchen stove on which she was cooking, despite the heat of that sultry Sunday. He had been due to leave for work on Monday morning, but his hacking coughs rasped through the little house and he was ordered to stay in bed. I had never before seen him in such lacklustre spirits and went around on tiptoe, wondering if death might be going to smite our family a second time. At length when this fear was confided to my mother, she laughed.

"Dinna be daft," she admonished. "Yer fayther's got a bad cold. Right enough, he's making a muckle fuss aboot it, just like a man. It's an awfu' wise thing the Good Lord didna arrange fer men tae have the babies, else their screams would scare the light right oot o' the full moon!"

Bird Box Hats

Our first summer in Red Deer in 1918, there was a laden patch of saskatoon berries just south of the hospital. At that time lard was sold in three-pound pails, pails that had lids and bail wire handles. Neighborhood boys tied empty ones to their waists with double wraps of binder twine, then went berrying. I loved picking saskatoons and gathered so many that my mother got upset.

"Dinna bring any more," she grumped at me. "I've made preserves, stewed them with rhubarb, and eaten them raw 'til oor teeth are blue. Yer brothers're sick o' them, so am I, and yer fayther's only home at weekends and he's wantin' a change too. Dinna pick more."

"But great clusters're going to waste up there."

She passed a fretful hand across her forehead as though not caring, then reconsidered. The word 'waste' had scored a major point.

"A-weel, doon the street there's a wummon with no man nor boy tae pick berries fer her; if ye must go a-pickin', tak' her a pailful."

She turned back to her baking and I climbed the hill eagerly to refill the lard pail. The widow lady answered my back door knock and viewed the brimming pailful with suspicion.

"How much are you asking?"

"They're free. I just like picking."

She smiled at me, emptied the pail into a bowl, rinsed my con-

tainer clean and wiped it dry.

"If you like picking, I like canning. Bring me all you can and I'll pay five cents for each pail from now on."

"But—"

"Don't argue. Besides, I'll be getting a bargain."

She bought eight pails from me and a friend of hers bought four more. My mother was pleased at my accumulation of coins; the next time I was with her on a shopping trip she bought me a small penknife.

"That's from yer berry money," she told me and I felt suitably rewarded. Not only did I enjoy seeking out the plump saskatoons, but there were patches of raspberries on hillsides, while the largest wild gooseberries I ever saw ripened on a shady bank of a CPR right-of-way near home.

My love of gathering nature's fruits survived the years. There was one memorable outing to Northey Flats the second summer of marriage to Marjorie. She had "the girls" in that afternoon and it chanced I had finished the final draft of a story to be mailed to a boys' magazine nicely named "The Open Road."

"Go fishing," Marjorie suggested.

Off I went, knapsack on my back and fishing rod poked up from it as I rode the bicycle along intervening trails, parked it in a thicket, then walked a fenceline bisecting two grainfields and went down a tree-lined path to a sparkling bend of the river. Three goldeyes were bamboozled by my homemade flies. After they were scaled, cleaned, and packed, I switched tackle and trolled a weighted lure through the deepest hole of the backwater. Two medium-sized walleyes sacrificed themselves, the best pan-fish our stream offered. Yet fishing time had been brief, the afternoon sun still soared high and home would be crowded with tea-drinkers. I had brought along a berry pail and four clean cotton bags. Sugar was sold in ten pound bags, the cloth containers much prized as carry-alls by fishermen and berry pickers.

Within hearing of the river's murmur and the low gabbling of ducks feeding in a shallows downstream, I moved quietly from cranberry bush to bush. These translucent berries were borne on low shrubs, not the moss variety of the foothills nor the large handfuls of the highbush type. One pailful required an hour to collect, whereupon the bagged berries were cached with my gear and I climbed a sunny ridge to a saskatoon patch. Three pailfuls soon bulged another sugar sack. I then sought gooseberries, without any luck except for a mouthful. Raspberries were too squishy for bike transport, while it was early in the season for chokecherries. Restlessly I prowled the forest byways eating a dewberry here, a woodland strawberry there, once pausing to admire a belated stand of white ladyslippers.

The final time I spent behind a juniper screen to watch a goose, gander, and four goslings on the water. These were the big Canadas, and they were ducking their beaks down to the river's floor to feed on snails. Frequently they came ashore to preen, sometimes flapping their wings appraisingly as though testing to learn if the moult was all over. At length the gander ventured farther up the bank to nibble on grass, grabbed an insect, then poised abruptly with head cocked because I had squashed a thirsty mosquito and the tiny sound had alerted him.

"Ger," the gander muttered.

The single note must have been important, because the goose and gosling heads were instantly raised in wariness. The gander went slowly, with dignity in spite of the undeniable waddle of its progress, back down the shore and eased into the water without a splash. All six of them floated there a long moment.

The goose murmured "Her-oop," in a troubled manner.

"Onk," replied the gander.

The goslings kept silent, but they immediately formed a single line of swimmers behind the goose, the gander bringing up the rear as guard. Without more goosey comment they swam upstream and around the bend. After they were out of sight, I gave another blood-satiated mosquito an executioner's chop, rubbed the swelling its proboscis had caused, then stood and stretched my cramped limbs. The sun had shifted far enough over to end the afternoon and I started the homeward journey. All but one of the girls had gone; that one was Wyn, a dear friend who had been invited to stay for supper.

"Now you've got a choice," Marjorie offered her after viewing my spoils. "Fried walleye with saskatoons for dessert, or potato salad and cake I made earlier?"

"Please, fish and berries," Wyn said.

"What about you, Nobby?"

"I'll have everything."

The berry-picking craze stayed with me. We have a dozen highbush cranberry shrubs scattered around the meadow; in top bearing years they yield two waterpails full of scarlet fruit. There are some who claim these fruits have the same odour as dirty socks.

• • •

Bird boxes get cleaned, repaired, then covered every autumn, an interesting chore with many surprises. Sadly, there is usually one dead tree swallow to be found, perhaps the puniest member of a clutch and forgotten after other members had flown. Successful boxes have all their grass and feather linings matted down to a caked hardness almost glued to the box floors. The green moss chickadees use for lining rarely retains any of its original colour, becoming a faded gray by the time the puffed out, larger-than-parents young leave the nest. Partly for decoration, partly for amusement, we cap most boxes with feminine headgear bought at the Salvation Army thrift shop, hats too decrepit for decent looks on people yet with a lingering allure frequently enhanced by bunches of synthetic fruits or a spray of artificial flowers.

"Why the hats?" visitors invariably ask.

"Each one has its crown stuffed with crumpled paper inside a waterproof bag. We think it makes the boxes cooler during the hotter days of summer, perhaps it helps keep them warmer on rainy days." Then we laugh and add: "Besides, they look funny."

One hat was sweat-stained and deeply creased, a cowboy creation that had about it an aroma so strong that, while the tree swallows perched under it experimentally, none deemed it a suitable haven for a nest site until it had seasoned three long years. Sometimes there is a brilliantly coloured hat that lights up part of the meadow. Those swathed in lace-like materials have to be severely trimmed, to prevent the entanglement of swallow feet. Our daughter Rondo regularly haunts the Edmonton Symphony Orchestra's annual rummage sale on the lookout for ancient hats of both gender, then carries them home to us on her next holiday weekend. We always reserve a special box for the Symphony Hat. Perhaps there is an echo of fine music tucked in such chapeaux, as they are attractive to the birds and have always provided favourite nesting sites.

Twenty years ago we gloried in having 50 pairs of tree swallows housed in boxes, but numbers have dwindled with the passage of time. Our boxes have been ready and waiting. It is just that wintering habitats of the swallow family have been badly reduced of late. We had mountain bluebirds in perimeter boxes for a number of years; they still come each springtime to explore the possibilities. Yet when a pair attempts to occupy a meadow box, the earlier settled tree swallows dive at them so aggressively that the exasperated bluebirds leave. Alarm shrieks of flocked tree swallows easily penetrate house walls. Such screeches send us running outside to see if it is a sharp-shinned hawk or a Cooper's that has tried to raid the sanctuary. The whole nesting colony of swallows careen madly after it and predator hawks are rarely successful here because of the swallows' watchfulness and fearless attacks. Only sharp-shinned, Cooper's, and goshawk accipiters give the otherwise beneficial hawk family a bad name.

"Marjorie, bring the camera," I shout if anything unusual is found during a cleaning spree. A brown bat tumbled out of one box when I raised the front panel, fluttering down to rest spread-winged on the grass. The bat stopped long enough to pose for its picture, then crept its way by wing-hook claws a few hops before spreading the leathery vanes and flying off into the screening forest.

Sometimes Mourning Cloak butterflies are found in the autumnal cleaning ritual, the beautiful insects having sought hideouts in which to spend the winter. These and the tortoise-shell butterflies frequently survive the cold months in hidden niches and emerge in springtime for a few days of erratic outings. Dusty miller moths are common in boxes, fat fellows that clumsily resent the rush of light. There is always an abundance of spiders, ranging from small crawlers up to the gangling daddy-long-legs. Not many times, but often enough to be noteworthy, a box will contain the paper and waxy remains of a wasp nest. Twice there has been the evidence of a bumble bee colony, but more often defunct bumblers may be found among the boxes' contents.

"Come see."

This particular box was stuffed full of bread crumbs, fragments of suet, and a handful of sunflower seeds. Filled right up to the entry hole, yet not noticed until cleaning time.

"A squirrel's cache, isn't it?"

"Yes, but since we haven't seen a red around by day, this may be the horde of a flying squirrel."

"Perhaps the one that bumped our window screen a couple of nights ago."

We never welcome squirrels around the feeders because of their bullying attitude toward smaller birds. If a red squirrel ventures near the bird box area during the nesting season, angry ruckus is raised not only by the tree swallows, but quickly joined by scolding robins, protests of chipping sparrows, ticking juncoes, and sharp whistles of red-eyed vireos. Squirrels are regarded by all such nesters as egg robbers and fledgling eaters.

Some hats covering our boxes are now ten years old, twenty if the original wearers' time is added. When colours fade and contours sag, a hat is removed and another installed to replace it. Until recently this has been done with increasing reluctance, as ladies' hats are difficult to acquire because of todays' styles of fancy hair-dos and valiant bare-headedness during all seasons. Only four 'new' ones had been in reserve. When this was mentioned to Gladys, she snatched off husband Henry's hat and said:

"Take it. It's time he bought a new one."

Henry accepted the loss of his tweed with tolerant grace. In fact, the next time they came for a visit he donated a gardening hat he had decided to replace. When Marjorie took a jar of jelly to an ailing friend one day and spoke about our hatted boxes, the patient perked up. She roused to ransack a storage closet and triumphantly emerged to proffer three 'oldies'. Therefore we now have seven hats on hand, one a flaring straw with a red plastic arrow pierced through its crown in belligerent defiance of good taste. I wonder if tree swallows would deign to perch on that arrow, or should I snip it off before mounting it on a box?

"Leave it on," advised Rondo.

"I'm undecided," Marjorie commented.

"It looks cute," Rondo added.

None-the-less, I shall probably remove the offending arrow before that particular hat is put out next spring.

When all boxes have been cleaned, dark green garbage bags are slithered over each as protection against winter winds and snows. The bottom open end of each bag is secured with a wrap of string tied around the supporting metal fence post. Later, back at the house staring out at the shuttered boxes, it struck us that they resemble a numerous array of cancelled car parking meters.

A facetious friend asked:

"How much was the fine?"

Unaccustomed as I Was

In earlier years there were invitations to speak at service club meetings, get-togethers of farmers and Rotarians, a convention of Women's Institute ladies, girl guide or boy scout leaders wanting tours through the Gaetz Lakes Sanctuary with their groups, and invitations to rural community halls. One wintry night when I was due to speak to a Home and School gathering at Delburne, an old farmer climbed out of a truck next to my car and glanced in surprise at the tightly jammed parking space.

"Lots of curious people here tonight, same as me."

"It looks that way."

"How far'd you come, stranger?"

"About twenty miles."

"Well, I've driven over thirty miles to hear this guy talk. They tell me the damn fool even likes hawks."

When I laughed and explained that I was the fool under discussion, he mumbled an apology and started to get back into his truck. It took persuasion to convince him that I had heard much worse said of me before he could be coaxed into the hall to mingle with his neighbors.

School teachers often telephoned and requested a natural history half hour in their classrooms, question and answer sessions with no

preparations necessary. Their students' queries were wide ranging in topic matter and occasionally startling, such as an earnest question from a Grade 3 boy:

"Do dragon-flies sew up lips of boys who tell lies?"

A better poser came from a girl whose grandmother remembered finding a phoebe's nest fastened to a bolt head underneath a creek bridge, the query being:

"What happened to that bridge?"

"It was smashed apart and washed away by high water."

There were many floods of our river and Waskasoo and Piper Creeks, peaking to alarming heights during the 1920's and 30's before those streams trickled down to present day size. Some years the river's spring ice jammed near the united creek mouths and the latters' brown waters backed up more than half a mile into the town, covering the place where bowling greens and an ice skating oval are located today. The flood lapped behind the sacred precincts of Gaetz Memorial Church, which was at that time the handsome brick structure later gutted by fire and replaced with a steep-roofed modern building of imposing bulk. The water was knee deep in the black birch hollows stretched between the church and the Central School hill where children used to slide on their sleighs at recess time.

Children asked: "What happened to rabbits at flood time?"

They swam clear and scampered off to the hillsides, though many mice and bushy-tailed Franklin's gophers and others of their ilk were drowned in their dens. Beavers and muskrats revelled in the high waters, while flocks of ducks came with outstretched webs and down-curved wings to swoop into these new ponds in search of food. Not many birds had nested among the drowned shrubs by the time of April floods, though bluejays and robins had started in tree crotches out of reach of rising waters. Most of the ground nesting migrants were just newly arrived from wintering quarters and not in immediate danger.

The flip-flopping of childrens' minds always kept me pleasantly alert. Once after a chat about the habits of toads, a girl waved her hand and asked:

"What happened to the shack where they stored dynamite for

blasting out sandstone for buildings?''

'They' had stopped building with sandstone because stone masons were scarce and, besides, a brickyard had started. A second yard came into productive competition soon after, as subsoil clays were excellent for brick making. A lumbering boom upriver around 1910 ended the brick mansion period, when shiplap, attractive outer siding, and V-joint for inside finishing became available from every lumberyard and carpenters were soon expert at putting up framed structures. Besides, two-by-four studs gave air space insulation, impossible to achieve with solid brick walls. The dynamite shack connected with the sandstone quarry industry served a second round of usefulness as a farm granary.

"Did you see any bluebirds, back then?''

A large flock arrived in the family yard in the midst of a 1920 May snowstorm. Perhaps the birds were attracted to our place by the sight of many boxes reared up on poles for their special use, also for the needs of tree swallows and purple martins. When the exhausted bluebirds began hopping from snowy branch to branch in a desperate hunt for food, my mother and father helped me cut raw bacon into small pieces, made crumbs out of bread loaves, sacrificed a whole batch of oven-fresh biscuits and raided our chickens' chop bag to help soothe the wild birds' hunger. The bluebirds actually snatched worms from my fingers as fast as I could dig them clear of the loam. The upturned earth seemed very black, when viewed against the stark white of six inches of new fallen snow.

All members of the flock could not crowd into my waiting bird boxes to spend the night, for there were far too many birds to fit the accommodations. I placed wooden and cardboard boxes upside down on the shanty-style roof of our chicken coop, propped the ends open to permit easy entry, and surplus birds gratefully huddled into these makeshift quarters. We anticipated that the flock would be just as hungry when morning came, so before bedtime I was dispatched among the sparse neighbors to tell them about the starving plight of this large band of sky-blue mountain bluebirds. People gave me trimmings of stews, raw hamburger, heels of bread and batches of stale cookies. At daybreak the birds emerged from bird houses and from upturned boxes, flying to the clothes line and lilac bushes and still bewildered by the deep snow lying even more thickly around. They greeted the dawn with a multitude of soft warbling whistles, a delightful symphony of bird music, and came most trustingly close to feed on our offerings and newly dug worms spread on the re-scraped clearing at the edge of the garden.

"Ahhhh!" breathed the listening children. "Wish we could've been there!"

A girl asked what it was like when the flock flew away.

"I wasn't there because I had to hurry off to school a mile away, only to be told that school had been cancelled because of the storm. By the time I reached home again only a dozen bluebirds remained. The thaw had already started and the others had scattered away."

"Where did they go?"

"Some to farm fields north to Edmonton and beyond, many must have gone eastward to house yards and farm plots around Stettler and Camrose, others might have flown west past Sylvan Lake towards Rocky Mountain House."

"Did you see big flocks like that every spring?"

"Oh, no. Usually we saw only one male bluebird in late March or early April, and the sight cheered us into thinking that perhaps the winter was really going to end after all. A mountain bluebird is very beautiful when seen against the backdrop of shrinking drab snow. Much later on, after Marjorie and I were married, another spring flock hurtled down out of a stormy sky to our secluded garden patch, maybe once again drawn by the many bird boxes easily seen from above. This time we were better prepared for them, because we not only had more bird houses, but we had bored entry holes under the eaves of our own and my parents' front porches and these provided shelter places for birds at emergency times. There must have been around five hundred birds in the 1920 flock, under three hundred in this second 1937 crowd. In the morning the migrants flew off and were gone, except for six staying on to claim nesting sites in our boxes. By the way, how many of you have built bird boxes this spring?"

There was a shocked silence. The room teacher, who happened

to be the school principal, cleared his throat brusquely.

"Class, we'll soon remedy that, won't we? Every boy will be expected to build a box during this coming week and bring it here Friday morning to be inspected. I suggest you girls persuade your fathers to help you build boxes, too." He turned to me. "If you write the proper dimensions on the blackboard, we'd be grateful."

One frantic hand waved in the air, the boy blushing with embarrassment when acknowledged.

"I know where there's an old bird house with its roof off. If I patched that up, could it be mine?"

The children were dismayed to learn that domestic cats were among the birds' worst enemies, therefore they were urged to put their new bird houses well out of reach of pussy cats.

"Oh, my poor Silky!" cried one girl.

Belling their cats might help, as the tinkling might slow down a stalking cat long enough to let a young bird escape from the reaching talons. They asked:

"Which bird has the finest song?"

W-e-e-l-l-l-l. Always count on those two flute masters, hermit and olive-backed thrushes, also, in bygone days the cheerful heartiness of western meadow larks singing from atop every fifth power pole. Plus the exquisite purity of the white-throated sparrow's song and the equal loveliness of the chickadees' serenades, the bubbling joy of ruby-crowned kinglets, the softer but haunting notes of the Townsend's solitaire, and the comforting repetitions of the veery thrush. I fondly recalled the Sprague's pipits high-sky whistlings, once a thrill of every June. If any of the children lived near one of the two city creeks, or not far from the Gaetz Sanctuary, they would still be able to hear the whu-whu-whuing of Wilson's snipe every May morning and evening. They volunteered that they knew and loved the honkings of geese, one boy enthusiastically adding that he had often seen a whooping crane.

"It comes to wade in our part of the creek all summer long."

"Perhaps it isn't a crane," I tried to be diplomatic. "Your teacher will certainly remember part of a poem that goes: 'I come from haunts of coot and hern, I make a sudden sally'?"

"Oh, yes, Tennyson," smiled the teacher.

"Well, Jack can wave a friendly hand at the great blue heron next time he sees it on the creek."

"Are coots just mud hens?" a girl asked. "My mother calls them that. We drove out to Slack's Slough last Sunday afternoon and saw a lot of them."

"When next you go there, carry binoculars with you and look for small, stubby ducks swimming near the green rushes not far out from shore. Look at their beaks, and if you see one that is bright blue and the bird's head part is white with a black crown and the body a cinnamon shade, then you'll be seeing that comical clown of duckdom, the ruddy duck drake."

"One of grand-dad's friends has a red car that's called The Ruddy Duck."

"I know that friend, too."

● ● ●

School classes became my favourite audiences in public speaking time. There were the freshness of young upturned faces, the happy appreciation of any funny incident of nature, the keen competition to think up the next question, their beams of pleasure if they could get me to close with a story about pioneers.

Women's Institute meetings were always the best organized and conducted. The ladies did not even change expressions one hot afternoon when all the screened windows were wide open and just outside in the farmyard, the hired man dropped a heavy whippletree on his foot and uttered some blistering words of exclamation. At those same farm home meeting places sometimes the lady in charge would ask if they might attend to their business routines first and dispose of correspondence before hearing my talk. This gave me a chance to wander along the nearest creeklet, bushland, or slough edge. Several times I forgot the meeting and walked too far, and would be recalled to order by an echoing 'Ha-lllllooooooo!' from a distant house.

Of the men's groups, Rotarians were the best behaved and easiest to please if I took care to observe their strict rule of getting it all said within fifteen minutes. They told me they had work to do, though rarely did they understand what I was doing was an intensified form of work too. Boards of Trade and Chambers of Commerce are evening affairs after banquets, and no speaker worth hearing will eat much before giving a talk. The curse of banquet evenings was the local politician, enamoured of a captive audience to extol whatever his or her party had done in years past and promising much more, going on and on while the too polite chairman leaned back and occasionally slept peacefully throughout the droning. Once there were not one but two politicians, each wanting to add a few more words after too many 'lastlies'. The crowd had come especially to hear about an historic project dear to their hearts and mine, but I was not formally introduced to that audience until twenty minutes to eleven after a banquet that started at six p.m..

There were frantic times when a program arranger would telephone in panic to say that their speaker had cancelled because of illness. Would I please do their club one last favour and come at once to fill in? One excited fellow forgot to mention the meeting place and there were three false entries before I found their new rendezvous. One of my strangest experiences came when I was asked to address a student group at a religious college. The teacher in charge rose as I entered, asked all present to bow their heads and close their eyes, whereupon he prayed aloud and at considerable length, closing with a blessing for everyone present—

"...including our speaker, and make his words good."

Chickadees and Wilbur

O ne early May afternoon a few years back when the wind had gone down, Marjorie and I went out to sit on the front porch for a breather after lunch. The stillness that had followed the blow emphasized the quantity of bird song all around, the warbles of purple finches predominating because they were the most abundant species settled close to the house. There were also the unpretentious solos of juncoes, the lisping of tree swallows flying above, the sermon of a song sparrow's homily near the garden, and the pleasant comfort of a robin's roundelay.

"What's that chickadee doing?" Marjorie asked, indicating one of the black-capped birds we had cherished so dearly throughout winter feeding months. "It's got a beakful of something."

We watched the little bird hesitate on a twig of mountain ash, before it made a swoop into a bird box set near a clump of pincherry.

"That's where a pair nested a year ago."

The male of the pair came to peer at us from a cut-leaf elder nearby, inspected us briefly and flew over to a small spruce next the lawn. The bird that had been in the box came to the top board of the fence, scratched the base of its beak with a claw, then dropped to the ground on our side of the white-painted boards. There was a small depression in shadow and we could only see the top of its head, but

we caught glimpses of quick up and down jerks of movement. The bird flew up to the top board with a blob that looked like a green mustache at the end of its stubby beak. One glance around, then it flew directly to the partially leaf-screened box in the cherry shrub. The male followed a short distance behind, not uttering a note but obviously wanting to watch all that was going on.

"He's riding escort duty," said Marjorie. "The female must have just dropped the stuff inside and popped out at once, because here they come again."

We almost ignored the gulls' cries overhead, the soaring Swainson's hawk, the insect-like buzz of clay-coloured sparrows, harsh cries of bluejays, and serenades of many other species in our concentration on the two blackcaps. Back and forth went the female, busy at gathering the green stuff we knew to be fragments of moss—a poor commentary on the state of our lawn. Each time her consort flew or perched nearby, both birds so intent on their duties that neither uttered a note during this ten minute session. At length the female stayed inside the box for a short time, returned to the fence board above the treasure-trove of nesting material and preened herself all over with careful deliberation. When this was complete, she flew off to one of the Heyer apple trees in the garden with the male following. Soon both birds were exploring the insect contents of the numerous flower buds covering the tree, taking a rest from box stuffing for the time being.

"It'll be an easy one to watch from the front window," Marjorie said, pleased. "Before we go back to work ourselves, shall we go along the bush trail to the other chickadee stronghold?"

A week earlier we had been fascinated by the industry of a chickadee pecking at the rotten socket where a poplar branch had broken off. Beakful after beakful of wood dust was delved out and with a twist of the head, tossed away. Even as we watched that first time, the bird had scooped out enough of the rotted wood to make a hole large enough to hide its head. Still the pecking went on, now the deeper digs causing the worker to rear back and sometimes leave the stump to rid itself of a larger fragment. Meanwhile the companion bird was twittering its cheery tsee-tsee notes above us, fearless of us but watchful too. At no time did the delving bird get any relief from the work while we were there, so different from nuthatch behavior. Another time we had watched a pair of nuthatches at a similar task; while one bird pecked out the nest excavation, the other bird foraged around for food and brought beakfuls of tiny insects every few minutes to give to its hard working mate.

"Let's go onto the ridge to see if the buffalo beans are in flower." They were. Gray curls of wormwood sage had sprouted too and saskatoon blossoms were sprinkled graciously along the top ridge and down into the more fertile parts of the hillside. The winter had been hard on evergreens; it had started early with heavy and killing frosts, provided little snow cover and lasted five months. Many of the native junipers were brown of needle and some of the spruces looked frazzled on outer branches and tips. But beside the bush path grew sturdy leaves of bunchberry, that diminutive relative of British Columbia's flowering dogwood. The ubiquitous dandelions had found a foothold, while fronds of meadow rue were more advanced than other plants. By moving aside leaf mould, we saw the veined shoots of wild sarsaparilla, the black-seeded ginseng of the west.

Following a circuitous route back to the house, a robin chirped its annoyance at us for rounding a corner too quickly. Its feathers glistened with water from the galvanized paddling pool. We had interrupted its bath.

"Remember Wilbur?" asked Marjorie.

Seasons ago when putting up more robin nesting platforms, I nailed one outside and above our bedroom wall. A pair gratefully accepted this as a safe homesite, well up from the ground and screened from view by branches and leaves of a decorative lilac. We watched the nest making procedure with amusement as the robins carried globs of assorted grass and twig particles to the shelf, tucked the fragments together in a mass nest before lining the structure with beakfuls of dirt moistened into mud by dunking it in their drinking pan. We laughed when the female, a vigorous individual we named Maud, settled herself into the mud lining and huffled around in a circle, pressing herself firmly against the nest walls to smooth out and form the interior cup before the final lining of softer grass. It was pleasant, morning and evening, to hear Wilbur utter his territorial declarations of musical pride of the new location.

Our troubles then started.

The nest shelf was about five feet above our bed level. There was the inner house wall of plaster, plyboard, air space, more plyboard sheeting, cedar siding, and an outer coating of vinyl siding. All this piled up to a generous eight inches in thickness. Quite sufficient, we thought, to insulate us from outdoors. Maud took up her throne position and laid her first egg. Wonderful enough, until the second, third, and fourth were deposited in swift succession. With restless beak and undecided mind, Maud began turning and rearranging the clutch and muttered something like this:

"Wilbur, it's been a chilly morning and the egg shells are cold, so cold my tummy feathers may be frosted. Come relieve me, will you? ... Wilbur? ... WILBUR! ... That pompous brick-fronted strutter, enjoying the last rays of the setting sun up there and me stuck on these clammy eggs ... Wilbur! Come Take a Turn! ! !"

Through the open window we could hear Wilbur's joyous praise of seasonal bliss, paying absolutely no notice to Maud. Fretfully, she began turning the eggs again, this action tight against the house and growing louder every moment. The wall seemed to have become a drum skin with Marjorie and me inside. We were forced to listen to every beak poke and shove as Maud kept complaining.

"There's no warm side to these blue ovals of ice. I'm hungry, too, and I need a break. Take a turn, Wilbur? ... Oh, drat. I'll just go catch a worm and have a wash-up. WILBUR! ! Listen to me, you vain-glorious little pigeon-sized turkey, come down outta that tree this second!"

Wilbur did stop his song long enough to perch near the lilac and keep a watch out for accipiters. We were sure of this, because we left our books and hurried from bed to watch Maud dig out some worms, indulge herself in a splashy bath, dipping down and up to swallow long draughts of water from the deeper end of the paddling pool. She next flew to the top of a fence post, rearranged a tail feather, nuzzled a beak under one wing at a time, probed her oil-gland and preened her plumage with all the fussiness of a ballet dancer putting on make-up. Wilbur remained silent throughout this procedure, having flown to the roof top to get a better view of the premises. Maud, relying on his wariness, went trotting across the lawn once more and found herself a snaky dew-worm, which she chopped into three portions before gulping. She appeared to smack her beak in enjoyment before giving herself a final settling huffle and returning to the nest on the house wall. We went back to bed, chuckling about all these doings but glad to resume our reading.

All went well until our real bedtime, when lights were put out and we wriggled against pillows to compose ourselves for sleep.

"Strike!" yelped Maud.

She had decided to play bowls with her eggs. The walls vibrated with the energy of her activities, with now and then a snide remark about Wilbur and his callousness regarding the whole affair, his stubborn refusal to take any time at brooding, and his general uselessness when it came to domestic chores. He had, meanwhile, shushed his singing a half-hour after sunset and presumably was perched somewhere out there in the gloaming, perhaps in the shadowy branch of a spruce tree back of the garage. In any case, it was the last we heard from Wilbur that night, but not from his mate.

How could Maud bowl in the dark; how did she keep score? We felt sure she was rolling those eggs back and forth strenuously enough to crack the shells, yet the simple looking blue things had their own inner strength and resisted all her persistent efforts. When she finally settled down for a nap and let silence reign near our buffeted ears, the clock dial revealed that it was 1:30 a.m. of a May night. Her bowling maneuvers had aroused us enough to make the brewing of cups of soothing camomile tea seem appropriate. We looked out at the luminous stars. Orion's sword belt was distinctive, the Big Dipper pointed to Polaris off to the north, and when we stepped out onto the back porch we could see the large W of Cassiopia on the opposite side of the Dipper. Far off we heard the lowing of cattle, the scolding bark of a farm dog, the drone of a car speeding alone on the night road.

"Time for bed again."

We settled down and slept. Maud became restless just after four o'clock in the still dim morning and hoisted those eggs around like a cement mixer working on boulders. She must have moved one from each corner over to the opposite niche, crouched on them to brood for a whisk of a second, then made up her so-called mind that they were better off the way she had them before. The wham-bam of tossing them hither and yon was repeated with great gusto all over again. By this time there was the merest hint of a yellow dawn over thataway, enough to arouse Wilbur. He took up his position in the lilac right outside the open bedroom window and at that early hour so close to our barely rested ears, his usually melodious notes sounded a wee bit piercing. Maud responded by engaging him in companionable conversation.

"Wilbur, here I've cuddled and maybe coddled these eggs all night long, and you'd think they'd have the decency to radiate a little warm appreciation. But no. Take a turn and spell me off, Wilbur ... Ah, there he goes off to that tree to sing his song over and over. Really, I've had it up to my chinny-chucker with his too-loot, too-loo, cheer-up and so on. Oh, my, the tedium of expectant motherhood!"

We snatched another hour's sleep when she went off to hunt for breakfast. Wilbur remained quiet throughout this interval while the clutch of eggs beyond the wall maintained their own brooding silence. Not for long. Shortly after they emerged from the shells, those fledglings cheeped, yapped, then bellowed for sustenance. They were never satisfied, no matter how often they were stuffed with worms. Occasionally Maud and Wilbur took time out to chase any crow or magpie that ventured upon the scene, and they became positively hysterical when a neighbor's cat sauntered within half a mile of the nest itself. All the while, heedless of external dangers, the lusty young yelped 'More! MORE!!!!' Our bedroom wall boomed with bird-thunder all those lengthy days and half the nights.

As soon as the assorted Junioresses and Juniors left the nest, I got out a ladder and moved that nest-shelf to the back wall of the garage, where it remains out of sight and almost out of hearing.

Moose in the Sanctuary

A cow moose became lonely in the Gaetz Sanctuary one June day during the mid-1930's. Red Deer had a population of around 3500 people then resident in and around the town valley, but none were abroad when the moose decided on a change of scene. She ambled along deserted streets at four o'clock that summer's dawn, and it is conceivable that she found the gravelled roads annoying to her hooves. A wide lawn bordered by tasty looking shrubbery seemed inviting, with the extra bonus of promising greenery next the house. She fed contentedly for a while, her large ears flagged as strident voices issued from a window. The people within the bedroom had roused early and were quarreling over some domestic botheration, their voices sharp with argument.

The cow stepped closer, curious about the source of the disturbance. The bedroom window was already half open, but feeling the heat of the dispute the husband now got out of bed and flung it wider. Then he turned and wagged an admonishing finger at his wife to emphasize a different point of view. The lady ignored him as she suddenly sat bolt upright in bed, fluttered her eyelids in shock, and uttered a shriek before collapsing under the covers. The man spun around and stood transfixed: a cow moose's head seen at close range inside a room must be an appallingly ugly sight.

"Holy mackerel!" He ran to the bathroom and locked himself in.

Not reassured by this reception the cow started to withdraw her head, at which moment the window curtains tangled on her big ears. She waggled her formidable snout at them, the vigor of her movement causing the curtains to rip off their rod and crash down upon her.

"Aaaaaauuuuuuoooooouuuuhhhhhh!" rumbled the moose.

She backed away just as the wife revived. The woman took another incredulous peak at the window and fainted a second time. Her husband, hearing his mate's gasp of despair, armed himself with a toilet plunger and ventured back. Relieved to see that the window was now empty, he crossed to it and stared out. The back end of the moose retreating across the lawn, with lacy curtains draped inartistically over her head and high humped shoulders, was not the most comforting sight after an already unpromising start to an otherwise beautiful morning.

"We need a drink!" announced the man, and forthwith plied himself and wife with full tumblers of raw spirits. They tried to tell one another what each had seen, got bogged down in exaggeration of the horror of their shocks, so they stopped babbling and drank more whisky. Later in the forenoon, relatives called on the couple. They were still garbed in pyjamas and kept trying to extract one more drop from a completely empty quart bottle.

"Was bigger'n a horsh," the husband slurred.

"Its nose seemed a whole block long," she said.

"I was right up close," the man added, measuring with his hands apart. "I felt my hair stand up, stiffer'n a poker."

Naturally the relatives believed that the weird apparition had come out of that empty bottle, and said so. With tremendous effort, the besotted pair made another attempt to convince them otherwise and became quite maudlin when their true stories were jeered. Doubts began to assail the stricken pair. In growing confusion they wondered if the early morning events had not been the lingering aftermath of a truly horrendous nightmare.

"Your dreams came out of that bottle," asserted the relatives.

Finally the pair nodded their heads in agreement with this more plausible explanation of their frightful experience.

"If tha's the case," said the man, not bothering to stifle a hiccup. "I'll never drink again—neverrrr!"

"Me too," his wife moaned.

To cap it all, they kept that promise. Years later the sober man told me the whole remarkable story and said some of the happenings must have been amusing, though not at the time.

Later, in the early 1940's, a pair of young bull moose took up residence in the Sanctuary. The under water vegetation at Second Lake provided them with succulent nourishment throughout the open weather, while forage of black birch, poplar, and willow twigs found in lowlands between lakes satisfied them for most of the winter. They had almost exhausted the available browse by January and became restless during a thaw. In the dark of night the two bulls, probably twin brothers, left the region and crossed vacant lots to the banks of Waskasoo Creek. They followed it sporadically until its twisting course may have confused them. At this stage they climbed a slope back of the fair grounds, meandering up over-grown remains of Roche Hill roadway. Reaching the toplands, the moose struck across a grainfield toward the dense cover of the Bower Woods. There they spent the rest of the winter, returning to the Sanctuary in the spring.

All these roamings left tracks which I followed with avid fascination to reconstruct their journeyings. Phil Galbraith, the local newspaper editor, had asked me to contribute an occasional nature article to his weekly, yet I had no wish to publicize the fact that two nearly full grown bull moose were dividing their time between Gaetz Lakes and the Bower Woods. Instead, I wrote about varieties of berry shrubs in the Sanctuary, the bark circling antics of a brown creeper there, even tried a little promotion on coyotes' worth by totalling a foraging animal's kill of destructive rodents after following its spoor for an hour.

Joe Cardinal was the game warden of our district at the time and we had become friends. One spring day when he came for a visit, he told me that he had just seen the tracks of two moose not far from the entry of our lane.

"They're not more than two days old, either. Rather odd, right here on the outskirts of town."

I nodded, and he glanced at me.

"You've seen them, too?"

"Are you going to spread word about moose being close to town?"

"No, of course not. I thought it'd be interesting to track them and find out where they're going. Or have you done that?"

"I've watched them for over a year. Right now they're in the deep woodlands back of Second Lake. They spent all last summer there and half the winter, then moved over to Charlie Bower's woods for a while. They returned to the Sanctuary a couple of days ago."

"You tight-lipped old rascal," Joe laughed. "Come show me and we'll share the fun of keeping tabs on them."

From then on we exchanged news about the moose movements. That second summer they left Second Lake and for a spell roamed the river wilds as far downstream as Northey land. The animals waded the river once to wander the wooded part of Three Mile Bend. When that palled they returned to the comparative security of the Sanctuary to eat water plants again. Even that 230-acre region became cramped for their maturing activities; one final time they crossed the river and climbed the Convent Hills. There, of an August morning, a man saw them and rushed to The Advocate to relay the news. The paper printed his excited account. Two days after the story appeared, Joe Cardinal's eyes were sombre when he called on me.

"They're dead," he announced. "Some nut shot both when they were in a West Park field. Shot them and left them, wanton killing for killing's sake. I'm disgusted."

So was I.

Later, before Marjorie and I were considering a move from town to our present location, another moose incident developed. Mrs. Jack Teasdale telephoned to ask if I would like to have a mounted moosehead. She wished to dispose of the antlered animal heads which had hung on the walls of her late husband's butcher shop. I had instant recall of the glassy-eyed trophies that loomed so huge in the meat store where our family had dealt for years.

"I've sold the elk and deer heads, but the moose— Would you take it?"

"No thanks, Mrs. Teasdale."

"Do you know anyone who would care to have it?"

It was not a question that could be easily answered on the spur of a moment. None of my friends' homes had room for the massive head of a bull moose. Instead, I suggested she get in touch with the local Fish and Game Association.

"You do it for me. Tell them I'll let them have it real cheap."

"I thought you were trying to give it away?"

"So I was, but it should be worth something to an organization. Try for fifty dollars."

"Mrs. Teasdale, nobody's going to pay money for that old head."

"Ohhh? In that case, say they can have it free, but they've got to come and get it."

One of my friends was an official of the association. When I telephoned him about the head he muttered a strong word, then said something about having known her husband. He supposed a favour was due that memory.

"But what on earth can we do with it?"

"Isn't your annual Smoker due in a couple of weeks?"

"Yes, and we've got you down for a speech, even though you don't smoke. What's the Smoker got to do with it?"

"Tickets are numbered, right? . . . Well, draw a stub and give the moose head to the unlucky holder of that number."

"Fine idea. I'll go pick it up and store the wretched thing in my garage until the Smoker."

The first man whose number was drawn refused to accept that monstrous trophy which expanded ponderously across two supporting chairs on the platform. A second draw was held, the winner promptly donating the head back to the club. The chairman pleaded for a volunteer to cart away the unwanted souvenir. The last I heard, the old moose head was resting comfortably in the Red Deer Dump.

• • •

During the early 1950's there were many work-party outings to the Gaetz Sanctuary. Thirty school boys from Grade 5 and 6 classrooms—and one most helpful teen-aged girl—accompanied me there on Saturday mornings. They helped clear litter off the paths, hauled logs to the public picnic spot in preparation for family wiener roasts of spring and summer, another time putting up bird boxes.

"Why here in the woodlands?" Doris whispered an aside. "Bluebirds and tree swallows won't come in here, will they?"

The boxes were being nailed at whatever heights the boys could reach with short ladders, fastened on dead trees and stumps not far from the main path. I had to wait until they were all busy before telling Doris that a few pairs of chickadees might use the boxes.

"The chief idea is to convince visitors that this is a sanctuary. Bird boxes may get the message across, even if they're not too practical in here. In any case, the boys phoned and offered to build the boxes, so how could I refuse?"

She nodded her blond head.

"It's a sort of public relations stunt."

Doris had phrased my thoughts in current jargon. The boys had toiled over their rough and ready boxes, the better ones having had parental help during construction. We spent a long morning erecting them at intervals, and the effect of the multi-hued boxes varying in size from wren boxes to cumbersome flicker houses, added a picturesque feature to the paths.

"Well, birds, it's all yours," said Bill, the oldest boy present and most expert with a hammer. "Hey, could we go exploring now?"

They had earned a diversion. I vetoed the notion of going to Second Lake where a doe was biding her time in a copse near the farther lake, and the first waterfowl migrants were nervously settling in. The faint marks of the long-ago Indian wagon trail were still etched through poplar woods where I believed intrusion at this season could do no harm. But halfway along, a ruffed grouse flushed up beside the track to disclose her clutch of eleven eggs. There were many pleased exclamations over this discovery, also many promises not to tell anyone.

Next day when I returned alone to check on the nest, at a distance through my binoculars there was no sign of the grouse. Instead, there was the bad omen of flies hovering over the nest spot. Close inspection revealed the imprint of a boy's shoe that had been stamped down to rupture all eggs. When I met Doris on the town streets a few days later and told her, that poised young lady broke down and wept.

"I could strangle all boys," she said fiercely through her tears. Years later she must have revised her opinion on one at least, because she married a forester. When she last visited us, she spoke most fondly of their isolated home in the distant mountains.

Ruffed grouse are scarce at our country location now. Years back a drummer paraded on a log within view of the garden, throbbing out the pulse beat with stiffly arched wings at intervals throughout the days and nights of April. Shortly after, the bright eyes of a setting female were glimpsed near a favorite path. I turned and retreated, not venturing that way again until the brooding time had passed. Marjorie accompanied me when we considered it safe to walk that path once more, and at one part of it an indignant lady grouse clucked furiously at us. She rushed forward with an elaborate pretense of broken wings, a disjointed tail, and produced hisses between fretful clucks. We caught the merest glimpse of several chicks, which scattered in a rush before suddenly blending into the surroundings and keeping still.

"Now, Mama," Marjorie said soothingly. "We'll leave."

We rejoiced in the success of that particular nest. Even though the young were now hatched and mobile, Papa drummed on for another full month. In autumn, Papa or perhaps one of the brood's young cocks mounted the same log, strode back and forth a while then stopped pacing with its head cocked to one side. At last the tail made a downward twitch, the wings shot up and down, and the muffled thrum resounded through the woodlands once again. Perhaps just healthy exuberation?

• • •

During another work party at the Sanctuary a smaller crew of older boys, plus Doris, collected deadfalls on the main shore of First Lake. We used a Swede saw to cut them into short lengths, rolling them together until the logs formed squares, then spiked cross bars and fashioned three sturdy rafts. We wrapped baling wire around rectangular rocks, leaving a length on each as anchor wire, and positioned one rock-anchor on each raft. Bill Baile and Jimmy Seeter volunteered to pole them out into the water not too far from shore. Another and Jimmy's raft were anchored first, when Jimmy transferred to Bill's craft as passenger to be ferried back to land.

"I can shed my pants and pole this third one out and wade ashore after," Bill offered. "That is, if Doris will beat it for a while."

Doris smiled and agreed to retreat. I knew the mucky nature of the lake bottom and objected to Bill's plan.

"Instead, let's give it a heave-ho push."

"How'd we get the rock off to anchor it, that way?" Bill countered. "Let me have a try, wading from shore. Doris, beat it around the corner for a couple minutes."

After she had gone Bill shed his trousers and stepped into the water, shuddering as his bare feet sought a grip on the yielding bottom. He leaned on his rafting pole for support, nudging the raft ahead. When we watchers decided he had reached the prudential limit of distance, Bill balanced himself firmly before poking the pole at the perched stone. On the fourth try, a splash rewarded him and the raft bobbed gently at rest among the lily pads.

"All clear, Doris," I called after the boy had been cleaned off and donned his clothing again.

"Tell us, what'll nest on 'em?" Bill asked, pleased about launching the trio that had been patterned after my own boyhood nest rafts once moored on Second Lake.

"They'll supply home-sites for ducks. Perhaps grebes will claim that farthest one; if we're exceptionally lucky, a pair of honkers. Though it's doubtful that wary geese would settle so near the picnic spot."

"My father calls the middle of his bald spread his picnic spot," one youngster announced. We chuckled, sympathetically in my own case. The rest of the morning was spent gathering waste branches from the building site, these carried back to stack behind the double tables and benches of the picnic area. In the middle of the small clearing was the fire circle. It had been carefully boxed in with a ton of sand hauled by wheel barrow load after load from the roadway. Cement blocks framed the fire-place as an extra precaution against sparks endangering the surrounding forest.

• • •

On the stormy-skied day of October 7, 1985, Marjorie and I walked out to the mail box to post family letters. During the jaunt we sighted dozens of juncoes feeding on weedheads. A Swainson's hawk rode the wind and peered down in hopes of sighting an unwary mouse. There were many gabbling flocks of snow geese heading south, sometimes individual members performing that masterly slip-drop aerial trick as they changed to lower altitude levels to join another flock formation. When we got back to the house yard white flakes began slanting down, the fourth snowfall of this autumn.

"This may be true winter," Marjorie said. "Remember how early it came and stayed, last season?"

"I'd better go dig the last of the garden while the ground's still bare," I responded, and got a shovel. The snow swirled thickly around me as the tool delved and turned, worms squirming away from the sleek blade. An eagle floated over, in complete command of all the gusty updrafts. Sight of it produced an angry squawk from a bluejay skulking among a last cluster of yellow poplar leaves. As the final shovelful of brown-black loam was turned over, the sun straggled out and decided to shine. Snow began melting as I cleaned the tool, oiled it, and wearily went back indoors.

Marjorie had tender fricaseed chicken and baked potatoes ready to serve, with the added attraction of the 'leavings' from her last batch of tomato relish. After Grace, when we glanced outside we caught a glimpse of different wings and forsook the meal for a quick trip to another window. The approaching winter's first pine grosbeaks had arrived and were warbling cheerfully.

The Paths

White-throated sparrows were among the first bird songsters of renown I recognized as a boy. They had been identified on the cottonwood tops at Prince's Island in Calgary. In season the beloved birds were usually within hearing from the treed slopes of Red Deer's hills, plentiful in the Bower Woods, always a pair or two in the Gaetz Sanctuary. I habitually wore work clothing and strong leather gloves when going there to patrol the public areas. Litter was a constant problem around the picnic spot, some of it filthy. Usually three or four benches had been moved, their boards mended or re-painted, sometimes a picnic table had to be sheeted over. My rough clothing caused a comment one evening when a father and son came in for a stroll. The youngster ran up to me with a shout of greeting and a happy smile, whereupon the father sternly rebuked his boy.

"Come away from that dirty workman."

The child obeyed, while the father ignored me as he went haughtily past. Perhaps he did not even hear the glorious music of a hermit thrush as I raked more rubbish into a pile. Yet, this same person, as a member of an audience of business and professional men a week later, listened in rapt attention to my guest-appearance address on day-to-day happenings at the Sanctuary. Descriptions of dragon-fly nymphs catching mosquito larvae under water; big-eyed flying squirrels denned in an old stump; the delicate aroma of twin flowers blooming up a glen; the intricate weaving done by a hen oriole as she constructed her pouch nest hung from a poplar crotch. I took a sardonic pleasure in seeing his startled expression of recognition.

At our present home, one June day in 1982 while we were shopping in town, a maintenance man treated our house lawn with dandelion spray. When we returned the place reeked of fumes similar to the banned DDT stuff. One junco was dead, another dying, while a male white-throated sparrow was hopping blindly about, vainly trying to fly. Marjorie captured it and I rushed indoors to get supplies. There was a film coating its eyes which we swabbed off with a dab of cotton dipped in luke warm water. The bird's heart hammered wildly even though it sat quietly in the hand. We could find no broken bones nor evidence of feather damage. The eyes appeared to clear somewhat after the third gentle swabbing. It recognized the water we offered and drank deeply, after which we set the bird down on the feeding shelf with a fresh array of mixed seeds. The white-throat sat still for a moment, its eyes turning as though fully aware of us watching. Soon it pecked hungrily at the food. Perhaps the blindness had prevented it from feeding ever since the spraying took place several hours earlier.

"Will it recover?" Marjorie wondered as we entered the house.

As evening came on, the white-throat became restless. Other birds had come to the food mixture and our sufferer had made no protest about sharing the shelf with them, unlike its usual dominant behaviour. It was nearly dusk when the bird attempted flight, staggering at first but gaining confidence as it fluttered over the back lawn to reach the wooded shelter south of the well corner. We noted the twig where it perched and watched the sick bird's outline as night came on.

At last we saw its head rise and heard the silvery whistle. Long after the stars were out, the white-throat's song helped convince us that our patient had fully recovered. At dawn it was the first bird note to gladden our ears. The well corner birch tree became its favourite singing perch, while his mate nested on a red willow branch closer to the ground. Perhaps it was just our imaginations, yet we were sure that this particular white-throat remembered our restorative care. It fed contentedly near us as we moved about the house yard, watched without fuss as we replenished the drinking pans or placed more bread crumbs and seeds on the shelf. They raised a family of five healthy youngsters. When these had grown to independence, our bird paired again and another clutch of four young reached maturity.

"It's mid-August, and he's still singing," Marjorie exclaimed one evening as she jotted down the day's nature notes. "The other males that nested near have all stopped, but our bird is still celebrating."

Throughout September it stayed close to the feeding area. We saw the bird come to drink, bathe, and feed until the third week of October. A howling wind screamed over the river spruces one cloudy evening, by morning the land was sodden with rainy sleet. Many birds had migrated away from the miseries of that storm, and we believed our white-throat was among them. During the 1985 season just past we had five pairs of the species nesting nearby, their oft repeated territorial songs likened to melodious benedictions for us.

● ● ●

When we still lived in Red Deer, Jim Bower used to get his wife to dial our telephone number at irregular intervals throughout the year. When she was sure we were connected, she turned the instrument over to her husband.

"Nobby, there's a pretty weed out in my garden that's got clusters of bright red stuff growing along the stem. Any idea what it's called?"

"It might be strawberry blight," I replied, and waited until he thumbed through a weed manual and confirmed the guess.

"That's it, right enough. It looked good enough to eat, so I fed some to my wife and the hired man. They tell me it doesn't taste too bad, but I got to wondering. Is it poisonous?"

"Not so far as I know, but Mr. Bower..."

"Oh, I didn't feed 'em much. There's another matter I want to talk about. Last couple days, there's a batch of black earth mounds popping up all over my garden."

"Are you going to tell me you've got moles?"

"Well, what's your fancy name for them?"

"Nothing fancy, just pocket gophers."

"What about our real gophers?"

"The yellow flicker-tailed animals are book-known as Richardson's ground squirrels, but never mind. You want to get rid of the mound makers?"

"I sure do. They've chewed half a row of carrots and now a fresh hill's showed up near the peas."

"Try trapping. Dig a hole bisecting a tunnel, set a Number One with a lettuce leaf over the pan, cover the opening with tin or plyboard and shovel on earth to seal out light. I've caught six, one right after another that way, all instant kills with head catches."

There was a partial silence on the other end of the line while Mr. Bower chewed on his favourite confection, peanuts, which he bought by the bushel. Finally he cleared his throat and dismissed the trap suggestion.

"I'd hoped for a better notion. You think there's more than one animal involved?"

"Yes, at this time of year. Mr. Bower, how do you feel about using poison?... Then cut a couple of beets into small pieces and pour in enough poison to moisten."

"I follow you, so far, but how do I get 'em to eat the beets?"

"Use a sturdy stick about thumb thickness, prod the end around the edges of a mound until the earth yields easily and reveals the whereabouts of a tunnel. Widen the hole into the tunnel, drop in treated beets, then repeat the process around each mound until four or more tunnels have been dosed."

"How long before it works?"

"About two days. There's another faster method I haven't used, but my mechanic friends claim it's the quickest cure."

"What've mechanics got to do with such critters?"

"They've got backyard gardens, too. They borrow a flexible hose from the commercial garages where they work, attach one end to the muffler of a car, bury the other end in a pocket gopher tunnel and run the car motor for five minutes. Carbon monoxide fumes kill the pocket gophers.''

"That's better. I'll go try it with my tractor. By the way, when I next meet up with the strawberry blight stuff, I'll taste it myself. Okay, Nobby, thanks for advice on my moles.''

There was a mocking chuckle just before he hung up; obviously, to Mr. Bower the culprits were still moles. No use to explain that true moles are carnivorous, their main food being earthworms. Moles had not settled in the western prairies for the simple reason that their food supply was not here. According to history, the absence of worms was due to devastating prairie fires that often swept across huge tracts of our grasslands. Fires ignited by lightning, or escaped from Indian campfires. The tremendous surface heat generated by those vast fires was thought to have scorched out earthworms that ventured to colonize the region during past centuries. When homesteaders came, they were surprised by the lack of worms but soon imported them willy-nilly clinging to the roots of nursery stock brought in from the east and south.

How to account for thick layers of loam the pioneers found ready for their ploughs, loam formed without the inexorable earth-moving abilities of productive worms? Well, remember the multiple den cast-ups of ground squirrels, prairie dogs, digs of coyotes, kit foxes, badgers and swarming mice. Remember sixty million bison and their droppings. Remember the billions of push-up mounds and long airy tunnels provided by those energetic vegetarians, pocket gophers; they were among the busiest loam-makers of the west.

After my chat with Mr. Bower, I headed off to Gaetz Lakes once more. We think the attractions of our present country home may be due to its variation of meadowland, berry and ornamental shrubbery, native poplar and spruce woodlands, also the bordering stretch of the river. These all help make it a working sanctuary.

Years ago almost every farm was a refuge for wild things, there being rows of nest cover along fence lines dividing fields where shrubbery, willows and aspen prospered. When grain prices boomed, ruthless clearing became the rule. Chemical sprays and the wind-drift from it quickly destroyed fence row cover; indeed, many fences disappeared entirely as every inch of space was converted into cropland.

Even shelter belts left for cattle no longer attracted smaller birds, as magpies and crows settled in such copses. True, most farm homes today are pleasantly surrounded with shade trees and trimmed hedges which offer a last stand for songbirds. But in such small areas they must compete for nesting sites with ever increasing numbers of English sparrows and starlings that have always thrived around farm granaries and implement sheds and stock barns. The English sparrows and European starlings are hosts of encephalitis, the disease better known as sleeping sickness which is transmitted from the birds by mosquitoes. Having suffered from the after effects of that nasty illness for thirty years, I have no liking for either of the two imported birds brought to this continent by man around the 1890's.

During our town stay, interested friends and strangers brought us anything of a nature oddity that intrigued them. One time a thirty-pound puffball, often a dead bird picked up on a highway, occasionally an unusual butterfly or impressively large giant water beetle, even an albino muskrat. Once I had been off in Ottawa doing history research and arrived home from Calgary on what was then called the milk train. It reached Red Deer around three of a summer morning. I enjoyed the chance to stretch my legs and walked through the deserted streets, at last climbing the diagonal woodland path up to our hilltop home where I eased myself quietly into the dark house. Several days of train travel had exhausted me, yet at that moment sleep was less important than my ravenous hunger. In eager anticipation, I opened the fridge.

"Tomatoes, lettuce, celery," I muttered, shaking my head. I swung open the freeze compartment and saw a waxed paper parcel. "That'll be cheese. I'll make myself a fat cheese sandwich."

The parcel was taken to the counter, where I wondered at the thickness of the wrappings. The article did not feel right either, not firm enough to be an oblong of cheese. Hopefully I unravelled the last of the wrappings: in my hand was the frozen body of a very defunct pocket gopher. Marjorie had a note tucked next it.

Danny brought this. His cat dragged it in for breakfast.

Notice strong digging claws.

They were impressive. Thoughtfully I re-wrapped the little mammal in waxed paper, adding another layer for good measure, then the whole kaboodle was replaced in the freeze compartment for burial on the morrow. I had lost my craving for food. Instead, the kitchen light was dowsed and I moodily climbed the stairs to the upper rooms where other members of the family were fast asleep.

Marjorie was amused by my loss of appetite at 3:30 a.m.. In compensation, she prepared me a bountiful breakfast.

• • •

On this chilly 1985 morning of late October with the thermometer registering eight degrees of frost, winter birds have been whistling loudly. Piercing calls from evening grosbeaks, loud wheezes from Bohemian waxwings, conversational quankings from both the red- and white-breasted nuthatches—all coming to laden feeders. Chickadees seem to be everywhere, all but three juncoes have gone and today, the 26th, we saw a lingering robin. There were no hawks sighted during our morning walk, though we did hear many a 'thief' call from bluejays. We also heard the rising canary notes of pine siskins, but only sighted a disappointingly small group of redpolls. Perhaps oil exploration on their favourite Aleutian Isles nesting sites have reduced the numbers that migrate south for the winter months. A female pileated came to the suet, dislodging two of her smaller relatives, hairy and downy woodpeckers.

If the birds follow the pattern of other years, all day long they will converge on the feeding area to feast, drink the warmed water we put out, afterwards going to perch in the thick shelter of the well corner trees to digest awhile before partaking again. As yet we have not held seeds and fragments of walnuts in our fingers to coax the endearing black-capped and boreal chickadees closer. Other winters it became an established pattern; during one ten-minute interval on a cold day, the trusting mites took over two hundred sunflower seeds from my mittened palm. When a nuthatch hovered near the mitten the scolding chickadees alighted on my arms, shoulders, and cap peak to stay out of reach of the newcomer's sharp beak. The nuthatch

switched back to the suet and grumped plaintively when a bluejay swooped in to claim the lump for itself.

Standing still on that particular day chilled my feet right through the thick winter boots, so I dumped the rest of the seeds on the shelf and briskly walked the woodland paths. Many chickadees followed, fluttering ahead at times to alight on twigs and peer down hopefully. Half way around the circle path I yielded and got a container out of a parka pocket and presented more seeds. Three fed at once, a fourth became shy, and a fifth bird whistled the 'spring's coming' notes of April, the clear notes they offer at every season of the year. A brown creeper went like a furtive mouse up and around the scarred bark of an ancient blam. Farther on, a rasping sound drew my attention to a large spruce. Looking that way, I saw the distinctive markings of yet another species of woodpecker, a northern three-toed.

Mentally recording another first-sighting for the day, I remembered these same trails in the flush of early summer when perfumed chokecherry bloom had followed the white and gold tassels of saskatoon and there had been a teasing scent of silver willow on part of the path. Thirty different bird varieties could be spotted on such an outing, with over a hundred species for the full turn of the year. Flowers had then brightened the trails, despite the drought of early summer. Brown-eyed susans had prospered during the dry spell, though bergamot and hyssop had not. Bunchberry, spikenard, and Canada violets had all beautified the borders. Out on the sun-drenched ridge, goatsbeard had poked up its meagre yellow flowers, after which the inflated bouffant seedheads flourished from June to September in haphazard splendour.

Two Canada geese had nested on our part of the river shore, but golden-eye ducks, bobbing in numbers on the waters during May, had left our stretch to nest elsewhere. A pair of saw-whet owls occupied the large brown box hung above a ravine path, the male tolling faithfully night after night. As usual the meadow boxes had been busy with tree swallows, cedar waxwing clutches adorned honeysuckle and lilac bushes, while both red-eyed and warbling vireos had settled near. Mowing the grass was not practical during the drought. With the mowers quiet in the garage, plentiful ground nesters settled undisturbed anywhere they chose in grass clumps under the shrubs. Hummingbirds were always greedy for our nectar feed last summer, because most wild and domestic flowers lacked moisture. Hummers always seem curious about our doings, often buzzing our heads when we walk the circle and ridge paths. Marjorie believes they just want to know where we are going as bluebirds used to do, anytime we changed our daily routines.

"Remember the day the tank truck drove in? Bluebirds perched on the roof right above us and watched the whole procedure, their slurred notes repeated often and worried during that busy half-hour."

Both ruby- and golden-crowned kinglets had come that same day, assorted warblers, native sparrows, robins and others. All busy with either nest building or feeding young, but pausing in their duties to look in on the tanker. After everything was finished and twilight had arrived, dusty millers bumped our window screens beyond the lights. A bat moved in to thin them out and we could hear its high vocals. As night deepened, we appreciated the trill of a sora rail, the rustling whisper of elder leaves, while a blue heron flapped over out in the dark and cranked out a hoarse croak.

"Let's take a stroll before bedtime," Marjorie suggested.

Off we went through the woodlands, the worn paths faintly visible in the friendly dark. As we turned a bend, Marjorie pondered aloud.

"Should we plan any improvements for next year?"

For a moment I deliberated, then laughed.

"We really missed our big chance away back in the centennial year. That's when I wanted you to dig the Centennial Ditch eighty feet long, fifty wide, and forty deep. It would have made a lovely pond."

"The only tool offered was your long handled shovel," she retorted. "It wasn't really for the birds, either, because you wanted to plant fish in it."

"Shorebirds, ducks and geese would have been welcome to share it. Besides, at the time you approved of having tasty perch fillets every other breakfast. You could have asked your girl-friends for help."

"I remember all the men were keen on the idea of helping you keep the fish population from exploding, but nary a man wanted any part of the digging."

"Oh, when it came right down to finishing touches, I'd have been glad to square off the corners for you. It was mentioned as an inducement at the time, but you wouldn't start digging even when boundary lines were pegged out on the meadow."

She laughed.

"I'll admit the Centennial Ditch became the conversational topic of our year. Even our kids began asking worried questions in their letters—For a while, they thought you were serious."

"I was."

We resumed the walk. Our own sanctuary byways had become as familiar to us as Gaetz Lakes trails were to me during the long years of tending it. At the height of enthusiasm for that refuge, my writings about it encouraged other people and places to follow the example. During the peak of the boom, we knew of more than a score of widely scattered sanctuaries all sponsored by Red Deer's famous one. And now we have had our own for a couple of decades.

"Why so solemn, suddenly?" Marjorie asked.

"Just being grateful. Our home, our beautiful surroundings, our friendly birds. It's pretty marvelous."

She slipped a hand into mine before answering.

"Yes, I know. For more than fifty years, together we've followed pathways to paradise."

I said: "Amen."

Kerry Wood at the Gaetz Sanctuary entrance.

Writer and Naturalist, Kerry Wood, has been celebrating and protecting the Alberta environment during his long and prolific career. He was born in New York, of emigrating Scottish parents and moved to Red Deer as a youngster, via Ontario, Saskatchewan and southern Alberta. Mr. Wood has combined his two great loves, writing and naturalism, into a career that has seen him publish 6,200 short stories, 9,000 newspaper columns and 8,000 articles on natural history and Alberta heritage. He has also participated in over 4,000 radio and 600 television appearances, in more than 60 years as an Alberta writer.

Kerry Wood has published 20 books, among which *The Map Maker* and *The Great Chief* won Governor-General Awards in 1955 and 1957. Mr. Wood won the first ever Vicky Metcalf award in 1963 for "writing material inspirational to Canadian youth." He also won the Alberta Historical Award in 1965, an Honourary LLD from the University of Alberta in 1969 and an Alberta Achievement Award in 1975.

Canadian magazine credits include *Canadian Home Journal, Family Herald, Canadian Boy* and *Country Guide.* American magazines ranged from *Field and Stream, Fauna.* to *Boy's Life, Teens, Coronet* and *Reader's Digest.* British credits include *John O'London's Chambers Journal, Boys Own* and *Blackwoods.*

In recognition of his work as a naturalist, Kerry Wood, while still in his early teens, was appointed a Dominion Migratory Bird Officer. Perhaps the crowning recognition of his devotion to the environment is the establishment of The Kerry Wood Nature Centre, in Waskasoo Park, in Red Deer, Alberta. This honour is in recognition of Mr. Wood's work for the Gaetz Lakes Sanctuary and his role in the establishment of 26 wildlife sanctuaries in Western Canada. Kerry Wood has retired, with his wife Marjorie, to his acreage near Red Deer. They have three adult children.